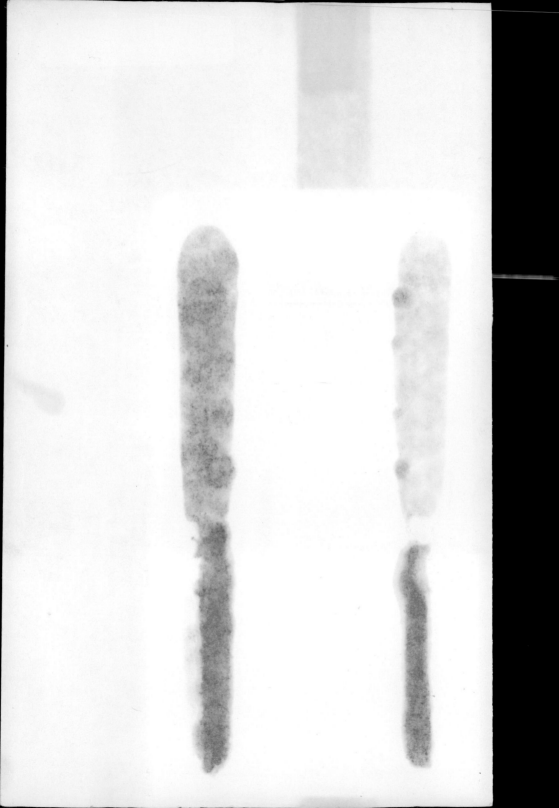

New York Cops Talk Back

NEW YORK COPS TALK BACK

A Study of a Beleaguered Minority

NICHOLAS ALEX

A Wiley-Interscience Publication
JOHN WILEY & SONS
New York • London • Sydney • Toronto

Library of Congress Cataloging in Publication Data:

Alex, Nicholas.
New York cops talk back: a study of a beleaguered
minority.

Includes bibliographical references and index.
1. New York (City)—Police—Attitudes. I. Title.

HV8148.N52A63   363.2′09747   76-1852
ISBN 0-471-02055-9
ISBN 0-471-02056-7 pbk.

Printed in the United States of America

10 9 8 7 6 5 4 3 2 1

To
Joseph Bensman

Contents

Stiffening of Standard Operating Procedure • Policemen
Under Surveillance • Guidelines and Restraints on Police
Behavior • Civilian Complaint Review Boards •
Restrictions on the Police Use of Firearms

The Knapp Commission and Police Corruption • Police
Vulnerability to the Opportunities to Be Corrupt •
Protective Practices in Dealing with Corruption

The Decline and Fall of the Police Reputation • The
Mortification of the Police Self • Police Are Scapegoats
for the Increase in Crime • The Police Are Hamstrung by
the Courts • The Policeman as Total Victim

Salt and Pepper Teams • The Militant Black Policeman •
Problems Caused by the Militancy of Black Policemen •
The Young Black Policeman Is a Special Adversary • The
Militancy of Black Police Leadership

Slowdowns • Trade Union Militancy • Political Thrashings

New York Cops Talk Back

Introduction

Ten years ago I began a study of black policemen in the Police Department of the City of New York.[1] In that study I discovered black policemen to be extremely competent professionals who used police work as one of the few channels available to them for social mobility. The Police Department, like other nondiscriminatory civil service bureaucracies, was able by its nondiscrimination to pick the best of a large population. But black policemen entered a world traditionally controlled by whites, many of whom had used police work as their own channel for mobility. Many white policemen felt that the police occupation was legitimately and properly reserved for their own ethnic groups. In their attempt to monopolize jobs and to keep whites in jobs considered to be "white," white policemen were often contemptuous of and aggressive toward blacks who became cops.

The new black policeman was thus subject to racial prejudice, isolation, segregation. His capacities were not fully realized within the department even though political superiors, as well as senior officials in the police department, made some attempts to upgrade black policemen to high-ranking uniformed positions and promotions to the Detective Bureau. The black policemen were not trusted

1

as partners, they were at times required to do the most dangerous work to prove to their white colleagues that they were "real" professionals, "real" men who were trustworthy and competent. They were expected to control the behavior of blacks both as "offenders" and in street demonstrations. Informally they felt required to prove their loyalty to the department by being overly strict, aggressive, and repressive to black offenders. They were also typically used as undercover agents to spy on black extremist groups suspected of starting race riots, and to take the pressure off white policemen in dealing with blacks.

This helped the Police Department in dealing with blacks, but it also exacerbated the situation of the black policeman; for the black community had an image of the police as a brutal and oppressive agency of a discriminatory, exploitative white establishment. The black policeman was thus seen as a tool of the repressive racial policy of white society. He legitimated white power, and generally did the dirty work of the economically, politically, and socially powerful— that is, he protected the white man's due process of law. Rejected, because of his occupation or profession by the community from which he came, he was also rejected by white society and a racially prejudiced, white-dominated police force. This rejection was all the more galling because most black policemen had developed an ideology, perhaps based on discrimination within the department, that their job was to mediate between the black community and the Police Department, to protect their community from police brutality. Yet with all this it seemed that the black policeman was doing a superior job.

Black in Blue seemed incomplete, however, since comparable data on the white policeman were not available. To find out to what extent and manner white policemen faced similar contemporary historical situations and cross pressures, this study was conceived. It is based on forty-two taped interviews with white policemen who work for the New York City Police Department. (For reasons of sampling, and to continue the earlier investigation, no policewomen were interviewed. Whether white and black policewomen share their male colleagues' perceptions of occupational roles and stresses must remain, at least for the present, an open question.) It asks the same basic questions asked in *Black in Blue:* why they became policemen, what they feel about their work, what the constraints are that affect what they do, how they are treated by their superiors, how they get along with their co-workers, how they see the community, and what separates them from others.

During the seven years between the beginnings of both studies the New York City Police Department has changed radically, however, making a difference in the attitudes of all groups. Economic and social change has occurred so rapidly that all established institutions and official ideologies that mediate between individuals and authority have been deeply challenged by counter-forces and counter-ideologies that demand a break with the old social order. The police as an institution is no longer pictured as the embodiment of society's values. In the late sixties and in the seventies, the Police Department has come under violent attack across the nation for brutality, racism, and oppression. The new visibility of these issues was dramatized in the demands for police review boards generated by the civil rights movement in the late sixties under the Lindsay Administration, which demanded to review, criticize, and control misuse of police powers by black minorities who believed they were victimized by such powers.[2]

The police have responded to this attack defensively. They have also begun to fight back against what they contend to be an impossible situation and the feeling that they are not getting enough consideration from the public. They have organized white ethnic police associations, and have loudly and militantly attacked their accusers through public demonstrations. They have discovered a sense of grievance in their work which has led them to make trade-union-like demands on the department and the municipal administration for higher pay and improved working conditions. Attempted job actions have caused them to confront their political and professional superiors. White policemen have found themselves in competition with firemen and sanitation workers over pay and working conditions and over the job-related conditions of danger and safety. They have found it necessary to defend in this competition the image of their manliness as expressed in the traditional image of the heroic policeman. Their entire occupational and ideological justification has thus come into question.

The attack on the police and the police counterattack were made both salient and extreme by race riots, changes in urban ethnic life, and the increased militancy of nationalistic organizations of blacks and Puerto Rican groups in the city. Support of white policemen was stimulated by the negative response of white ethnics to street riots and militancy, intermittent guerrilla warfare, and such issues as community control, welfare, scattered-site housing, student riots, "unequal distribution" of poverty funds, and by the outcry of white ethnics who see themselves as the victims of crime in the streets. The importance of these issues in the presidential campaigns in 1968 and 1972 may have contributed to the sense of moral righteousness one sees emerging in the counterattack of the white policeman.

During the period in which this study was undertaken, the police have also been subjected to investigation of their basic competence and honesty. The Knapp Commission Hearings of 1971 dashed the hopes lifted by the Patrolmen's Benevolent Association's successful campaign to defeat the New York City Police Civilian Review Board in 1966. The hearings also stimulated police defensiveness, resentment, and revolt. Perhaps the budgetary situation of New York City and other urban centers will take the ideological heat off the policeman, since criticism of their special claims to protect the community from crime and violence and to maintain "law and order" can be made in terms of fiscal rather than ideological necessities.

All these issues are explored in this study. They permeate the interviews and interlace with more conventional issues related to police work as a craft. The concluding chapter shows how these macroscopic issues are related to the particular professional issues of police work. An attempt will be made to explore not only the social psychology of police work, but the institutions that create and alter the special character of police work, and how these institutions affect the motivation, attitudes, beliefs, and world views of the policeman. The focus will ultimately be on how historical changes in the structure and climate of police work affect the procedures, motivations, and psychological tone of men whose traditional work habits and goals have been shattered by violent change. All this will be examined in the context of the Lindsay Administration, the internal changes and shake-ups brought to the organization and work styles of police work by former Police Commissioner Patrick V. Murphy, the Knapp Commission investigation into organized police corruption, and the increasing ability of black minorities to play balance of power politics in our central cities.

This book, then, is about the crisis experienced by the police as an occupational group, the historical circumstances in which their legitimacy and ideology are being challenged, and the counterattack of policemen who take pride in the traditional ways of doing their work. It deals with the decline and fall of police impermeability to outside control and intervention. And it addresses itself to the broader problem of questioning the legitimacy of all traditional institutions and ideologies in American society in an age of violent change and social crisis.

In sum, this is a study of beleaguered white policemen during a dramatic period of their history in New York City. The disintegration under pressure of police methods, prerogatives, autonomy, standards, and codes are described and analyzed. It is a study of what these men believe has happened to their work to bring this about, and to explain the discontents and demoralization generated by it. Above all it is a study of the psychological responses of policemen to a series of career defeats and betrayals brought about by societal change.

My methodology involved spending two years in the field with a tape recorder and talking to each police officer for one to three hours. An interview schedule was used treating their responses clinically and diagnostically, and problems of sampling common to all qualitative studies occurred.[3] Yet there was no real burden on my part to have policemen talk about their common experiences, feelings, and attitudes in a department undergoing radical changes. Interviewing policemen is like interviewing convicts in prison.[4] They are eager to make public their case against the injustices of the system; at the same time, they are counting the days before they return to civilian life.[5]

I am especially indebted to Joseph Bensman who suggested that I do the study, and who was always available for discussion and counsel. Out of gratitude, respect, and affection, this book is dedicated to him. I owe a deep debt to Arthur J. Vidich who generously gave his time and knowledge in reading, checking, and criticizing the manuscript in its several revisions, and who made many important suggestions for its improvement. Thanks to my friend Gerald Levy for an immense amount of help and encouragement in many ways. I am deeply grateful to Larry Mullane, Carleton Irish, John A. Williams, and Robert J. Raggi for all they did to help me in the early stages of my research, and for taking a personal interest in the study. My wife Deanne, provided considerable assistance and support from beginning to end. I also want to thank my daughter, Jenny, for respecting my need to work. I must also express my profound appreciation and thanks to the forty-two unnamed policemen who made this book possible.[6] A Herbert H. Lehman College Fellowship Award enabled me to complete this study.

NOTES

1. See Nicholas Alex, *Black in Blue: A Study of the Negro Policeman* (New York: Appleton-Century-Crofts, 1969).

2. Perspective on this ideological issue can be gained by reading Jewel Bellush and Stephen M. David, eds., *Race and Politics in New York City* (New York: Praeger, 1971), Chapter 3, "Police: The Civilian Review Board Controversy," pp. 59–97.

3. My aim in this study was not to obtain a true probability sample of all white policemen in the New York City police force, but rather to select a sufficiently diverse study population so that I could identify the range of problems that are indicative of the topic under study. To this end I recruited respondents from a variety of sources, relying not only on police contact sources, but on nonpolice sources as well. I was particularly successful in obtaining diversity with respect to ethnicity (the police are of Irish, Italian, Jewish, and German origin) ; age (fifteen are in their twenties, sixteen in their thirties, nine in their

forties, and two in their fifties) ; time on the job (from one to thirty-two years on the force) ; and the area in which they worked (precincts in Central Harlem; the West Side and Greenwich Village; the South Bronx; the Bedford-Stuyvesant area of Brooklyn; Queens and Staten Island).

4. See, for example, John Irwin's examination of the convict's perspective in *The Felon* (Englewood Cliffs, N.J.: Prentice-Hall, 1970), especially Chapter 4, "Looking Outside."

5. A typical comment: "I was with my wife a few weeks ago and we were in the car together, and a fellow in another car who was a policeman—I knew him very well since we had come in together as policemen—and he waved to me. And then I said, 'Hello, Joe.' And he held up some fingers, and he yelled out how many years he had left. He didn't ask me how I was. I hadn't seen him in some time. He just held out some fingers indicating the time he had left in the department. He just let me know he was counting the days. I saw another fellow today, and he asked me: 'How does it feel pulling time'? That's the feeling in the department. The men are counting the days. I count the days. I've got three and a half years to go. It's a little over a thousand days." (17)

6. To assure each police respondent's anonymity I have substituted a numerical code symbol in parenthesis after each quote.

1

The Motives for Choosing Police Work

A central problem in the study of black policemen was to explain how blacks had come to choose police work as a career. It was found that police work was a highly desirable occupation because alternatives of equal pay and job security were not available. As civil servants at a time when it was the active policy of city governments to increase recruitment of blacks into police work, black policemen could earn a relatively good income and have far better job security than offered by other possible jobs. Although police work was not principally valued for its own sake, given the situation of racial discrimination that faced most blacks, it was the best available choice.[1]

But it was assumed in the study of black policemen that the reasons that blacks gave for choosing police work would not necessarily apply to whites. What would apply to white policemen was a definite commitment to an image of police work as dispensing social services and safeguarding the rights of individuals, some intrinsic feeling of satisfaction that might be produced by the work itself, and an occupational history that would reflect a family tradition in police work. A certain amount of pride and identification of the white policeman with his job was assumed, a pride that would be accentuated and reinforced by the public ideology of the police officer as the guardian of law and order.

From the data to be presented two main points emerge. First, and contrary to my expectations, the motives of the white policeman for choosing police work seem little different from those of the black policeman: job security and relatively good income are emphasized by fourteen respondents. Second, eighteen of the forty-two white policemen interviewed *did* perceive and experience police work in the expected terms. Their orientation toward work is largely *social* as expressed in the needs for status, prestige, tradition, self-realization, and autonomy rather than, as in the case of the overwhelming majority of black policemen, economic. A typical example of this social or noneconomic orientation toward work follows.

POLICE-CAREER ORIENTED. Since white policemen identify themselves with the upholders of social order, their work expectations are of a social, moral, and positive kind. White ego-involvement in police work is strong: social recognition, achievement, challenge, and purpose in life are expected from the job, and are expected to be emotionally rewarding. Consequently, the meaning police work has for six respondents labeled "police-career oriented" is that of a central life interest:

> It was a boyhood ambition. As far as I can remember I always wanted to be a policeman. My eighth grade graduation book, where it says, occupation, well, it had police officer under my name. And as a boy, and getting older, I always thought the policeman was there to help people. At that time I thought there was a certain status to being a policeman in the community . . . . When I was a teenager I used to read everything that I could on narcotics. I would say that I am a buff who became a policeman. Most of my heroes were policemen when I grew up. Although my father wasn't a policeman, some of his friends were policemen and I admired them. (27)

Another policeman can scarcely contain his enthusiasm and identification with a time-honored tradition in police work:

I guess you can call it one of the classic cases—from knee-high
to a grasshopper I always wanted to be a police officer. I have
a couple of members of my family who are senior members of
the job right now. And it all started when I was a youth. There
were good cops in my neighborhood. These men were doing
a job the way they are screaming for professionalization today.
These men were real professionals! In the forties and fifties
these men were really good police officers. And I was so impressed with them that I decided at a very young age what I
wanted to do for a living—to make a life out of it. (20)

One police officer, a former seminarian, views his recruitment as a
return to the fold in which attachment to the business world is
rejected for idealistic dedication to serving the urban community.

I spent three years in the seminary in a monastic type of
existence from the ages of nineteen to twenty-two and then I
went into some IBM work. I came out of the army and went
into banking. And all of it was kind of sterile for me. And
the business life, the banking existence, seemed to me to be
pretty insipid, and I felt that there must be more to life. There
must be something more vital and more interesting to do in
the mainstream of life, especially in this city. I had a brother-
in-law who was a policeman and I began to listen to his war
stories and his experiences. And I decided that police work
would be more rewarding for me. I, quite frankly, lost a little
money when I joined the department. So I became a policeman
because of the subconscious desire. It came out of my feeling
of a vocation. . . . And the vocation, the kind of connotation of
a vocation, is beyond the professional idea—it goes much further. You know, it is something special. A policeman, whether
he realizes it or not, has perhaps the greatest vocation in an
urban society. (35)

This convert extols police work as a religious experience. Police
work is for him a source of emotionally significant experiences that
satisfy his expressive and affective needs; it is a source of moral
self-realization. Police work is therefore something special and valuable to society.

And every human need and every human crisis in this city gives
you the opportunity to be truly all things to all men. And the
result is that you get a tremendous amount of satisfaction out
of this work. . . . And there is a very definite idealism that is
required for this job. . . . And I have come to the conclusion
that if a policeman does not have a very fundamental moral
conviction or a fundamental religious conviction or at least
some humanistic convictions, he is not going to be terribly
successful. He doesn't see his role as a doer of good and a
helper of people. He sees his role solely as an enforcer of law.
If he sees himself as just an enforcer of laws, well, he is going
nowhere and he will become disappointed. (35)

This is not simply talk for its own sake. It is, I believe, an appeal
for social recognition that policemen are benign and helpful social
agents. It is an ideological strategy to overturn the traditional definition of the police as a punitive agency that is repressive and insensitive. By taking the view that policemen are dedicated social servants, and then building up a self-image around this theme, the
policeman validates his occupational status and legitimates it to the
public at large. Police work is an honorific occupation and an important mark of prestige insofar as the policeman is identified with
upholding law, order, and morality for the good of the community.
And all of the respondents above are interested in pursuing this
ideal.

Understandably, such a portrait of police devotion and virtue has
its appeal to policemen in the way they order their needs and expectations. However, we are uncomfortably close to the rhetoric of
police public relations, which is often the opposite of the view the
public holds of the police. To the public, the social expectations of
the police-career oriented cop smack of wishful thinking and flights
of fancy.

ACTION ORIENTED.[2] Another social orientation toward work is indicated by twelve respondents who view policing as active and
adventurous work.[3] Excitement and even manliness are associated

with the job—it is not like tending a machine in a factory or continuously filling out forms in an office. Police work is not routine. One is not fixed to the same spot but has changing horizons of work each day.

The element of variety. This was a big factor. Throughout my whole life I tried different types of employment even when I was a youngster. I always became bored, and it got down to a point where I was ineffective with routine and no change. So I found myself looking more and more for the variety of life so to speak. And it seemed to me that the Police Department offered this particular asset in employment. (20)

A highly decorated police officer in his early twenties shuns bland office work and loves a long, hard chase. Police work fulfills his need for dramatic crisis and miltary adventure.

The day I was appointed was, like, you know—like it all came together. Holy God, tomorrow I'm a cop and today I'm a pencil pushing accountant, which I didn't like. I couldn't sit behind the desk. . . . So the adventure is the big thing. That was the big thing about taking this job. I'm the kind of guy, if I was a millionaire and I wasn't married, I would probably have my own little army somewhere in the jungle of South America. This is the way I am. If I'm not out there with the trees and everything I'm not happy. I can't sit behind a desk and push a pencil all day long. I was offered a job about four years ago for twenty-five thousand dollars, and my wife said to me go right ahead—you know, it's your decision, what are you going to do. I said I'm not going to take it. I wouldn't be happy. . . . I couldn't see finding myself doing something that is day in and day out the same thing. It's another world here. I come to work in the morning and it's not the same every day. I mean there are certain routines on this job. It is the same office. You are in the same car with the same people. But every corner is another surprise. And that is the way I like it. I wouldn't have it any other way. (37)

The desire for action, adventure, and excitement combines with the need to break out of fixed routines or boring, uninteresting work rhythms. Thus all action seekers express negative attitudes toward the uniformity of repetitive work as a reason for selecting a police career.[4]

I had been working since I was ten years old. And of all the jobs that I ever had it was the most attractive job in terms of not being in a routine. And I didn't like clerical work. I wanted to be on the outside. (42)

I go back twenty years. Off the top of my head, trying to think back to give an explicit reason [for joining], I thought it was a job that was adventurous. A job that I wouldn't be bored at . . . . (13)

Splurges of activity, high excitement, even danger validate a sense of manliness. This manliness consists of working with or against human beings, rather than with inanimate objects or the manipulation of abstract symbols and words. Thus police work for the action-oriented is personalized.

Moreover, policemen wear militarylike uniforms, carry guns, and have the legal right to use violence in their work. This equipment is associated with manliness by one police officer:

I remember sitting at a restaurant and seeing policemen having their lunch and I saw their equipment and I was impressed with them. I was impressed with this impressive hardware. Not that I was interested in guns or anything but it was *manish*. . . (17)

"Manliness" may be crucial to the policeman because his working-class or lower middle-class background has socially insulated him from the prestige symbols available to a member of the middle-class. He knows that he cannot make the grade of middle-class occupations because of his limited education (the majority of New York City policemen are high school graduates) and, as we have seen, office jobs hold no attraction for him because of his need for "action." Hence he suffers relative status or prestige disabilities as a result of his social class origins. This means that his self-fulfillment and career expectations often differ from those of middle-class persons. The middle-class person wants to be creative, to be innovative, and emphasizes intelligence rather than brawn or manual skill. Blocked from these prestigious opportunities, the lower middle-class policeman seeks to establish his manliness through the nightstick and the gun, two of the few prestige symbols within his reach.[5]

One police officer suggests the interesting notion that the gun becomes the prestige vehicle through which the power of the police organization is somehow magically transferred to the individual:

A cop knows what he represents. A lot will tell you that they took the job for security. But also, so they could carry a gun. And they can shoot with it. So becoming a cop gives you instant self-respect. What do you do if someone is going to hurt you? You say, I don't care because my gang is bigger than yours. It gives you instant power. (4)

Manliness also carries with it the prestige of authority that police work legitimates. One police officer talks about the need for authority, and he identifies with it easily because authority inspires, commands, and elicits respect on the part of the audience:

It may have had a lot to do with my upbringing. . . . I was sort of like, you know, there is always one kid on the block who is the skinniest kid and the boys are always picking on him. I'm not saying that I was a mother's boy when I was a kid on the street. And maybe I felt that I needed to be the boss for a change. Joining the police is a way of getting it out of your system. You are the authoritarian for a change! You are telling people what to do instead of everybody telling you what to do. (37)

This image of the personal nature of police work rejects middle-class work, which is thought to be characterized by filling out forms and symbol manipulation. Thus a quality of lower-class romanticism and an idealization of the social rewards of becoming a policeman is expressed in the replies above insofar as policemen feel they have direct personal power over individuals; that is, they are free, autonomous, and masculine. Of course, the image of police work does not necessarily mesh with the reality. A lifetime of police work clearly involves a great deal of routine—directing traffic, covering assignments, checking out complaints, interviewing people at the scene of a crime, touring in a patrol car, walking a beat, or occupying a "fixed post." Then, too, there are the many hours when nothing happens on the job, or when the only things that happen have happened a thousand times before. The realities of police work also involve a vast amount of paper work, typing up reports, filing, taking phone calls, and keeping work schedules. Yet mistaken assumptions that they are free, autonomous, and masculine still serve to direct action-oriented policemen into channels of mobility, and to legitimate their crusading stance as admired agents of social order.

SOURCES OF POLICE IMAGES. Finding out where such images come from is important. For a very few, police work is a family tradition. Take, for example, the following two comments about family influences. The father's position in police work or other civil service job leads him to put pressure on the son to select police work as a career.

My father worked for the City of New York in Transit Authority, and he always told me it was a secure job. I wasn't really thinking of that too much but he prompted me to take the test. . . . And, another reason why I joined the Police Department is that my sister is a policewoman in California and so is her husband. And, you know, he said it was a pretty good job and everything, and both of them like the job very much. (14)

I joined the Police Department at an early age. I was twenty-one years old. My father was a policeman and I always had a liking towards cops. My father had something to do with it. He sort of pushed me to take the test. (21)

Mothers are in some cases more clearly a determiner of occupational choice. The interviews reveal that mothers frequently influence their sons' level of occupational interest. The sons acquire from their mothers a positive evaluation of police work as a civil service job and a reminder that police work is one of the best jobs available for a high school graduate without special skills or an aptitude for college work.

My father and brothers were policemen and my mother worked for the city. . . . My mother advised me to take the test because she told me that I had nothing to lose by it. . . . (You said that your mother advised you?) Yeah, she knew I wasn't going to college at that time so she felt that police work was a good job for me considering the education that I had. (9)

My mother was the one to make me take the test. . . . (What did your mother think was good about the job?) The security, the money, the benefits—the whole bit. I was thinking about the excitement of being a cop. Now, I am thinking of the benefits. Now that I am getting married the benefits are more important. (12)

My mother felt that the epitome of success was to be a cop or a priest. If you weren't a priest you should be a cop. This was the way Irish mothers were at that time. This was what they hoped and dreamed for their sons. (13)

One policeman, whose boyhood was spent in an Irish neighborhood in the Bronx, points to his family relationships. To better themselves, his brothers and friends left the services and turned to city employment.

My background—the Irish American family growing up in the Bronx was more or less—I wouldn't say expected of them—but more or less he saw his older brothers and friends becoming policemen. I happened to join in 1956 and a lot of my friends happened to join right after World War II. It seemed that everybody I knew that was in World War II either became a policeman or a fireman or a state trooper. (26)

Nevertheless, many police officers believe that Irish American families no longer pass on the civil service tradition to their sons. The interpersonal grid of a father, brother, or other relatives who are police officers and whose favorable view of police work may once have acted as a source of influence to bring others into the force is no longer operating as a major source of police recruitment. We cannot illustrate all of these statements, but have selected one that is typical.

There is no more recruiting from your own family. The average policeman doesn't want his son to become a policeman. He tries to get his son through college or to some technical trade and he avoids the Police Department. Years ago it was a big thing to get into the department. The bright young boy used to become a policeman. This is not true anymore. No one goes out and solicits some young fellow into the Police Department if he is a member of your family. You talk him into a job like sanitation which has less responsibility and the same money, or the Fire Department which is basically the same amount of money but the greater availability to moonlight. (33)

Another influence is the neighborhood policeman who serves as a folk model. A few respondents were inspired to become police officers as a result of identification with the qualities, function, or attributes exemplified by their neighborhood policemen. For example, one police officer reflects on the abstract ideal of character and behavior of the neighborhood policeman as more than life-sized— as a kind of mystic healer of community ills.

I was born and raised in Harlem, and the policemen that I knew were influential. They were the mark of authority, adventurous, stood alone. Anything that went wrong in the neighborhood they seemed to correct. He was a God—a miracle man. He was a guy who could prevent things from happening or could correct the wrongs. And seeing these guys operate the way they did—that impressed me! If I could go through life doing good—this is what I wanted to do. (13)

Policemen in the neighborhood are immediately visible figures of social order who offer young aspirants to the role a promise of such tangible rewards as power, authority, and social respect. All these serve as legitimating devices to produce a certain amount of pride in police work.

When I was a kid I used to see cops on patrol and you would be standing on the corner and they would pull you up and tell you to move on. You know, you figure that these guys have a little bit of authority. Like when you are young you figure the cop is the boss. You always looked up to a cop. They had the authority. You would see them with a gun. He would tell people to move. He stopped people. They stopped. I always thought of the cop as a good guy. And this was an important influence for me in taking the job. I had respect for the cop. (21)

What these responses suggest, therefore, is that white policemen have in fact been influenced to enter their present employment not for want of any real alternative, nor for economic motives, but rather as the result of their identification with the police officer in their neighboorhood as the upholder of law and order.

But for a larger group of policemen it is the mass media, particularly television, that helps produce these images of being upholders of order. Among the respondents who emphasized adventure, excitement, and lack of routine, television was an important influence.

I was very much impressed, corny as it may sound, with television police. (Television police?) Yeah, always seeing it on television. This impressed me. That is, the glamour, and the way they kept crime checked. They were publicly devoted guys. And with the cops and robbers thing—it was the biggest game you ever played when you were a kid. So I looked at the job from that angle. (25)

Well, when you are young you always see in the movies and television people with guns. You don't associate with those people but the gun has an interest. I know when everybody comes on the job they can't wait until they can carry the gun. But once you have it, it doesn't mean anything—it's like a part of you. It's not a big thing anymore. Anyhow, in answer to your question, you see cops in shoot-'em-ups on television and that has to be a factor for a lot of guys. (22)

Television policemen are synthetic substitutes for much of the complexity and ambiguity that we know characterizes police work. Yet television police dramas may serve as impersonal agencies of socialization by organizing and integrating the personal needs and values of individuals for adventure, excitement, glamour, meaningful work, and public devotion to the common good. Such a discovery has its appeal:

I became a cop because of the glamour, making arrests, enforcing the law, preventing crime—the type of things you watch on television and soon to be disillusioned. (12)

One police officer feels that "playing cop" is an all-American pastime fantasy, that television encourages everyone to become a kind of policeman. Television enhances and illuminates police prestige and reinforces the vigor and value of the police life-style. The police identity is strengthened through the seeming omnipresence and omnipotence of the medium:

Cops have a mystique because we get on television a lot. In every man there is this childhood thing about policemen. The cops and robbers thing. Everybody has it. . . . There is definitely this mystique and this idea of shoot-ups. You are doing a man's job. You are doing something very manly. If we analyze it we can say the cop is the total man. He can test all these manly characteristics. (35)

One of the major points of contention in the study of mass media has been whether television produces changes in attitudes, or whether it only reflects realities that already exist. If these policemen are sincere in their responses, television dramatizes and personifies ways of life and ways of work in sufficiently powerful terms to motivate at least some recruits to select police work. The same dynamics may operate for doctors, lawyers, and social workers.[6]

We shall find, however, that nothing is more frustrating and demoralizing to the young police officer than to hold an adventurous image of police work and to see himself driven further from it daily. It is a sad irony for the police officer to see police work becoming increasingly dull and bureaucratized without the advantages of a bureaucracy. I am not referring here to the advantages of security and the relatively high pay, but to rights, privileges, and exemptions that a bureaucracy can give; that is, the prestige, the power, and the freedom to express a certain autonomy in police work. Young men select police work because it means freedom from constrictions, restraints, and work routines. But the reality of police work reflects an increasingly constricting world. Thus, idealized police images generated by television necessarily lead to frustration and anxiety for the men who hold them.

SECURITY ORIENTED. My study of black policemen revealed that civil service security was a major attraction of police work. Fourteen white policemen indicated a similar motivation for entry into police work. These respondents saw in police work the opportunity for mobility to relatively safe havens—long-term jobs at relatively moderate pay. This underscores the striving working-class and lower middle-class backgrounds of most policemen. For families of these backgrounds, police work still has some virtues.

Poverty not only limits opportunities for jobs and life-chances, but it is a specific, frustrating, and personal experience that psychologically reinforces the need for economic security.[7] Thus economic problems become the context of personal needs for security. The following policeman reminds us that the person who comes from a poor working-class family is never free from the basic need for economic survival.

I would think that it was security. It was many things. But I think that at that time I came from a poor family where we used to eat onion sandwiches. We didn't have too much to eat at certain times. We went through the Depression. So I think that was really foremost. I would never be wealthy on this job but I wouldn't have to eat banana or mustard sandwiches. A lot of nights I used to dip the bread in the salad just to fill up. My family was on public assistance. And it was a hard time. The investigator used to come up and ask where did you get this and that and how come you are using so much ice in your ice box. (17)

For this man, anxiety over economic security was, therefore, the major factor in selecting a civil service job. What is not clear is the extent to which this anxiety prevented him from selecting other jobs.

Many of these men were also worried about their lack of a trade or skill or educational background.

Primarily when I was inducted into the Army in 1941 right after Pearl Harbor I had graduated from high school and I had no trade of any kind. And after spending four and a half years in the service, when I came out I was part of many thousands of veterans who were looking for a job and without a trade. My primary concern at the time was to obtain a position that would give me security. And when I was discharged I thought that the Police Department would be the best vocation in terms of security. . . . (24)

I had no trade, I had no profession. I had graduated from a vocational high school, which prepares you for nothing. So the money was good compared to what an unskilled man can get on the outside. (8)

Some men selected police work because they were sure of keeping the job. Economic security in these terms means job continuity.

At the time I was a machinist and the firm that I worked for wasn't doing too well and I was working only three days a week. I realized I would need some security and this job presented itself. (3)

I took it because of security. Prior to taking the test I worked for Republican Associates, a Farmingdale defense plant. I was married while I was working there and I got laid off on April Fool's day. Then I got a job through a friend of mine who was a shop steward of the sand hogs—they dig tunnels—where they were digging a sewage tunnel. And talking to the older men while I was on the job, I found out that this was a job where you worked six months and then they laid you off. So the guys told me to get out and I decided to take the police test. (6)

Job continuity also gives a man self-respect; he takes pride in his ability to support himself and his dependents. Pride is also expressed in the ability to meet self-imposed standards, to be constructive, and to hate futility.

I used to work for a machine shop. When they slowed down they laid you off. When they had work they kept you busy and would hire more guys. . . . I wanted something more steady. I must say this: I always took pride in the job that I did. I always wanted to do a good job. When I was laid off I couldn't take pride in the job anymore, and besides, I had a family to support. Then I applied to the Police Department. What attracted me was the security. It was a steady job. (1)

These responses show that money and security are positive factors in attracting men into police work. The new generation of police officers, on the whole, believes that police work is a job first and a public duty second. They are not particularly interested in or committed to the images of public service, police professionalism, and selfless bravery. They see themselves as working men and they want their money. They feel they deserve more money than people in the other uniformed services, and want enough money to meet the rising cost of living.

INDIFFERENTLY ORIENTED: OCCUPATIONAL DRIFT. Some respondents lack a positive image of police work; yet others were indifferent about becoming policemen. At the time of recruitment, ten respondents did not identify with the occupation, were not ready to accept the values and ideology attached to it, and were not prepared to model themselves on those already on the job. These policemen had no clear occupational commitments or preferences either to police work or to nonpolice work. They simply drifted into police work by a series of "accidents," chances, and unplanned decisions; they had made no clear-cut choice.[8]

The opportunity was there at the time I did become a policeman because they had the walk-in tests. And I was working as a truck driver before that. . . . I worked in the Telephone Company and I didn't like that. I had different other jobs, specifically labor-type jobs. So a friend of mine and I just decided to take the test. (Just like that?) Yeah. Just out of curiosity more than anything else. Just to see what the test was like. (30)

The typical indifferent tends to reject identification with the police model which promises (for the police-career and action oriented) authority, status, and prestige in exchange for loyalty and identification with its values. In so doing, the indifferent shows marked vocational apathy, lack of any internal direction, and limited aspirations.

(What was it about the job that attracted you?) I took the test with a friend of mine and I just took it. I never seriously considered joining the police although I guess I must have entertained some notions about it but nothing really serious, I never had any friends who were cops and I never had anyone in my family who was a cop. It just struck me that I might do

it, and when it came down to it, it was the only thing I could
do. I wanted to get married, and here it was, I was out of
school and no one wanted to give me a job. And the draft was
down my back and it came down to either one or the other.
And they just grabbed me first. Had I gotton a job someplace
else I would have been doing that. It was just the first thing
that came along. People used to say, why do you want to become
a cop for? And I really didn't know. (34)

Those who drifted into police work knew little or nothing about
the job. They did not acquire the ideology and values of police
work, nor were they influenced by family members, or by neighborhood policemen who served as models. Moreover, police work had
no intrinsic meaning or importance for these men; they made no
real effort to obtain an appointment to the department. They are
simply indifferent individuals whose reasons for becoming police
officers are gratuitous, impulsive, and accidental. Moreover, their
indifference is observed by them with detachment, without any sense
of personal involvment in their own decision making.

I don't know what kinds of answers you have gotten before but
I suppose they told you that they always wan'ed to be a cop.
When I graduated from high school—that's just what I had; a
high school diploma. And I didn't know what I was going to
do. I wasn't one of these guys who say I always wanted to be a
cop. I walked in and took the test and passed it. That was the
only desire that I had. I heard about the test and I said I would
take it—why not? (18)

Before I became a trainee, that is, a police trainee, working as
a clerk, I was working for construction. I worked in basement
waterproofing and I was going to high school at night. I only
needed three credits to graduate. They [police] called me in
and I became a police trainee in 1968. I was undecided on what
I really wanted to do or what I really wanted in life. I ran
around with a bunch of guys who figured that this was the last
thing I wanted to do. (Why is that?) Because I was the type
of kid who was always getting into trouble and never doing the

right thing. I guess I caused a lot of trouble. I suppose I was an average American kid you find today. The week before I was called by the police I was working in construction and I had a big accident. No one was hurt but because of it the boss fired me. I then worked for a gas station pumping gas. Then I got called by the Police Department. But I don't know if I would have joined the Police Department if I had not been fired from construction. (12)

But perhaps an objective reality governed even these "accidental" entries into police work. Since World War II the demand for police has almost always exceeded the supply. Pay rates and other inducements have made police work attractive. For those who could measure up to the existing standards or job qualifications, there are always opportunities for young men in police work.

And we can speculate that, for young men who had no clear-cut job choice or commitment to an occupation, the constant availability of jobs made police work attractive—applying required little effort and less motivation. In addition, the standards were less sharply defined than for much of the other work available to high school graduates who did not plan to go to college. Police work was a magnet for those with low motivation; it was easy to drift into the job by a series of changes, accidents, and fortuitous events since there was no strong pull in other directions. *Thus, what we call "drift" is simply the opportunity to get a job as a policeman but not the persistent opportunity to get other jobs.* This means that anyone who had the minimum qualifications or was "stuck" in some way could always fall into the one job that was open for him.

In the postwar period, then, several factors seem to govern the motivations of youth to choose police work. To repeat, a basic recruitment pattern of second-generation youth is from lower-class and lower middle-class families who stressed the economic advantages of police work. Like the black policeman, therefore, the white policeman finds police work attractive despite the many negative attributes they both see in the work. But unlike the black policeman, whose career alternatives were closed by racial and ethnic barriers, the white policeman contended with barriers that were primarily internal, personal, psychological, and motivational. These include a lack of any sharp occupational preferences or interests, lack of the chance to go to college, and the ease of entry that police work offered.

Nevertheless, our data also indicate that economic and indifferent orientations to work, notwithstanding, the white policemen's motives for entering police work are *less* connected to economic mobility than are black policemen's motives. The job is seen by almost half of our respondents as a possible source of satisfaction for authority, autonomy, deference, and prestige. Hence, the white policemen had higher expectations of *social* rather than economic rewards. Their self-identification as upholders of law and order was a powerful inducement to join the force.

Now that we have seen how policemen define their work at the point of entry, we can ask whether the job conforms, actually or symbolically, to their desire for job security, autonomy, status, prestige, and for the conditions they believe essential for good police work. Can policemen find these values, and indeed their identity, in their profession? The answers show that the realities of police-work fall far short of new recruits' expectations. What is admired and valued in police work is betrayed by the direction police work is taking. This frustration would seem to be at the root of police distress over and resentment toward the "decline in standards"—a frustration loudly voiced in the next chapter.

NOTES

1. See, for fuller discussion, my book *Black in Blue: A Study of the Negro Policeman* (New York: Appleton-Century-Crofts, 1969), especially Chapter 2, "The Recruitment of Negroes for Police Work."

2. The *term* "action" is from Herbert Gans's book, *The Urban Villagers: Group and Class in the Life of Italian-Americans* (New York: The Free Press, 1962). However, the *concept* "action," as I have applied it, has more in common with W. I. Thomas's "wish for new experience," and with F. Thrasher's treatment of this idea in his study of delinquent gangs, *The Gang* (Chicago: University of Chicago Press, first published 1927), Chapter 5, "The Quest for New Experience."

3. To be sure, some police-career oriented respondents also mentioned the need for "action" and adventure as reasons for selecting police work. But the action-oriented police officers, as a *type*, are not concerned with preparing themselves for an occupational status or career in police work, but are primarily interested with the "ideal" of action and the desire to escape from, or compensate for, routine monotonous jobs. Thus the presence in the interview material of this type of orientation is not an all-or-none affair, but simply one of emphasis.

4. Friedman reminds us that answers such as these need not be taken at face value, since criticism of the monotony of work in any particular case may also be sentimental ideology, or may conceal other job characteristics that workers find disagreeable, such as being on bad terms with a boss or employee or work group. See Georges Friedman, "Outline for a Psycho-Sociology of Assembly Line Work," *Human Organization*, Vol. 12, No. 4 (1954).

5. Some (by no means adequate) support for these generalizations concerning manliness can be found in T. Parson's "Age and Sex in the Social Structure of the United States"; also, "Certain Primary Sources and Patterns of Aggression in the Western World." Both are reprinted in Parsons, *Essays in Sociological Theory Pure and Applied* (Glencoe, Ill.: The Free Press, 1949).

6. For an interesting article on the power of television to influence occupational choice see Melvin L. DeFleur, "Occupational Roles as Portrayed on Television," *Public Opinion Quarterly* 28 (Spring 1964), pp. 57–74.

7. For additional evidence on the need for security as a function of lower socioeconomic levels, see Ann Roe, *The Psychology of Occupations* (New York: John Wiley & Sons, 1956), Chapter 3, "The Role of the Occupation in the Life of the Individual."

8. For a nice treatment of occupational indifference as a style of accomodation to work in bureaucratic settings, see Robert Presthus, *The Organizational Society* (New York: Vintage Books, 1965), Chapter 7, "Patterns of Accommodation: Indifferents."

2

The Resentments of White Policemen

One of the major policies of the Police Department is to develop morale among its members and to motivate those entering the field to accept the obligations of their profession. This policy promotes department efforts to upgrade entrance requirements, to raise standards of conduct, and to strengthen the special heroic qualities and skills of policemen.

To implement these goals, the Police Department has established the Police Academy; advanced training; the notion of a subsidized college education; in-service training to expunge racism in their ranks; lateral entry at middle and upper level jobs so that qualified civilians entering police work do not have to start at the bottom; and other elaborate programs to persuade blacks, Puerto Ricans, and whites to pursue police careers. All of these efforts are an attempt to justify an image of police work as special, "enlightened," and professional.

These programs will, it is hoped, make the work appear so attractive that better-qualified individuals enter the field. At the same time, they may be used to repair the sullied police image.

Some idea of what effect these programs have had on police recruits is in part answered in the previous chapter. If we combine the police-career oriented and the action-oriented policemen, almost half of the respondents in our study population were influenced by positive models of police work. But these models seem to have been generated by television and by neighborhood police heroes rather than by departmental public relations schemes. It should also be recalled that ten entrants to police work (those labeled "indifferently oriented") showed marked vocational apathy, and this sizable minority showed no motivation to become policemen or little internal direction beyond "some job." Furthermore, except during fiscal crises such as New York City is currently experiencing, the demand for recruits to police work has been greater than the supply during the post war period, and therefore availability of jobs probably has attracted more recruits than any efforts on the part of the Police Department.

Ideally, an occupation improves the quality of its personnel by making the pay, the nature of the work, or the prestige of the work so attractive that the number of persons seeking the occupation is greater than those who can be accepted. The existence of high standards makes the occupation doubly attractive because the potential candidates are selected after a series of sharp and competitive eliminations. Those who make it are the elect.

From our data two things are apparent. First, the oversupply of jobs not only undermines attempts to raise standards, but leaves policemen who are eventually appointed without a sense of accomplishment. They therefore develop resentment at the decline in standards and low morale. Second, the "decline in standards," far from being the cause of increasing resentment and disenchantment with the job, is rather a convenient phrase that white policemen seize upon to resist the integration of minorities into the police force. This resistance is articulated in statements about the decline in standards, not directly in statements against blacks and Puerto Ricans who are becoming co-workers. Anti-integration attitudes may be expressed in this indirect way because policemen believe that racial discrimination is morally wrong, because the policy of discrimination and overt exclusion is discredited by law, and very possibly because the average white policeman may recognize the legitimacy of the black protest for equal job opportunity. In any case, "decline in standards" becomes a strategy or code word to handle resentment and hostility in a socially acceptable way.

Yes, the standards have declined to the extent that I think it is ridiculous. It makes me feel that I no longer want to be associated with the Police Department or that I don't want to have anyone know that I am a policeman. Years ago, going back to the Police Department in 1947 and up to ten years ago, let us say 1957, is when this change began. This change started to come about and I then started to lose a lot of my ambition. (24)

They are undermining the force. The guy who wants to do a good job is disgusted. As long as they keep up the standards of the job—this is what is important. (11)

By the same token, policemen with high mobility orientations (like our police-career oriented) consider integration one of the most important causes of police debasement. These men become intolerant of any group that competes with them for the rewards of their social mobility or threatens their position as the established and time-honored group in the department. Underlying this anxiety appears to be resistance to social changes that are perceived as threatening to the security of their present position. These men are caught in a predicament. They proclaim that they are upholders of society, that they are committed to law and order, which they identify with their own success. But the definition breaks down when their enemy (blacks and Puerto Ricans) joins their ranks. To be truly upholders of law and order would require that they believe in democratic principles of justice and equality of all under the law, and act consistently with that belief. But to do this would require them to put aside their antipathies and become purely detached professionals.

But even the men who chose police work as a means to an economic end or who brought to their employment an indifferent attitude begin to experience qualities and values in police work that they had previously denied or to which they had been insensitive. The worker with low mobility orientations is suddenly reconstituted and transformed by his learning experiences on the job. In this he receives assistance from the Police Department, which inculcates in him a strong belief in the importance of his function. The effect of this dynamic is to allow the policeman to imagine better things of himself, and to provide him with a new rationalization of motives for entering police work. This improved image leads these men, too, to speak of the "decline in standards."

Our respondents are fully aware of the problem raised by low recruitment standards and low morale, and they speak of it in detail. What follows is a matrix of resentment against the "invasion" of disaffected minorities into the system of law enforcement as expressed in statements about declines in standards. The white police are hostile toward integration because blacks and Puerto Ricans threaten not only their established claims to the job, but also their social mobility.

THE DECLINE IN PHYSICAL REQUIREMENTS. In New York City, police candidates must now be sixty-seven inches tall. The eight policemen who mentioned this decrease in the height requirement all agreed that its purpose was to recruit more Spanish-speaking men, who could not meet the previous physical standards. Two of the respondents saw this as an advantage. One felt that it allowed all other ethnic groups that were disadvantaged by height requirements to now enter police work; the other argued that it was a way of alleviating the language barrier that exists between white policemen and the Spanish speaking community.

The Puerto Rican people are comparatively short. So if you want Puerto Rican cops you have to lower the standards to meet this population. However, I should add here that by lowering the standards for Puerto Rican cops they opened the job for all other ethnic groups that could not previously meet the height requirements. (6)

White cops and Puerto Ricans are immediately faced with a language barrier. The Puerto Rican cop knows the language and can talk to the people. From a practical point of view, from the point of view of police work, it is excellent police strategy because the Puerto Rican cop can establish the facts. (4)

However, two respondents are uncomfortably compliant to the change in height requirement because they feel that only tall policemen can perform their job effectively and with authority. Height is seen as having sensory and emotional attributes that gives the public the illusion that the police officer has authority and thereby deserves respect:

They lowered the height requirement to five feet seven inches. And they did this for the Puerto Ricans only. When I was in the Academy we had a lieutenant as an instructor and he had high standards when he picked partners for radio cars. You pick your own partner for radio car duty. And he wanted the biggest guy he could find. When he tells you to move, you move. A small guy will be challenged more than a bigger guy. (1)

In an effort to defend their prestige, white policemen discover the superiority of their physical qualifications for the job. Since the white policeman is closely identified with his occupation in his own mind, he begins to discover weaknesses in the physical characteristics of those who are not white.

One respondent goes so far as to suggest that a policeman who has the right body image can perform his job effectively even though he may be mentally limited. The short policeman, on the other hand, must compensate for his lack of stature by at least presenting a neat appearance. In other words, height becomes a distinctive symbol of prestige which tends to evoke a response from members of an audience:

Yes, physical standards have declined but the police officer has to represent a certain authoritarian figure. . . . You can have the dumbest cop around but if he is tall or if he comes in looking neat it makes a big difference to the citizen and how the citizen is going to respond to him. People will respect him. So the important thing is that if you are short, like the Puerto Rican, you should at least present a neat appearance to compensate for this. (7)

The other four ethnocentric policemen are strongly opposed to the change in physical requirements as a means of redressing racial disparity in police employment. One police officer puts the case quite bluntly, and we believe speaks for the other three, by supporting a *strict* enforcement of civil service standards and a rejection of the use of ethnic quotas and proportional representation:

Five or six years ago, to become a cop you had to be at least five foot nine. The standard came down to five seven because Puerto Ricans are smaller. This is a form of discrimination! Let me put it this way: I wanted to leave New York and I went to Florida in January and took the civil service test down there and I got a 91 on the test. This was in Dade County. About a month later I received a letter stating that I could not be favorably hired. The reasons they couldn't say in the letter. I believe that down South they are still prejudiced. And they are not going to hire Jews. . . . If a man is qualified he should be hired. In other words, just to pick a man for his race or his ethnic background is no good. Down South they keep you out because of your ethnic background, but up in New York they use it [race] to bring you in whether you are qualified or not. (25)

The lowering of physical requirements for police candidates has become police policy in cities other than New York. In Los Angeles, for example, dental, visual, and height-weight requirements were lowered for police and fire department recruits because seventy-one percent of 430 candidates were disqualified because they could not meet the existing physical standards.[1] More recently, the governor of Florida was so desperate to recruit blacks into the State Highway Patrol that he waived the weight restriction by thirty pounds.[2] What all this means, of course, is the abandonment or circumvention of the civil service system to recruit more blacks and Puerto Ricans for city jobs. What it means for whites is status defensiveness and resentment.

THE DECLINE IN WRITTEN TEST STANDARDS. A more salient issue among twenty-five policemen is the contention that the civil service written exam has been simplified, or test scores have been lowered or modified. Policemen feel that watering down test standards deprives them of any feeling of satisfaction or accomplishment, not to mention improved self-image, that comes from performing well in a competitive test situation.

> The tests are easier. The test I took, I took without studying. I never even looked at a book and I think I got an 88 without ever looking. It takes a little pride out of this job. (18)

> I work with a fellow who told me . . . he is a pretty intelligent fellow although he was at the bottom half of his graduating class—I suppose he didn't apply himself—anyhow, you know those walk-in tests, well, he walks in with two other fellows who just came along for the ride. And they said they would take the test too. They got about 92 on the test. Now these two guys are not cops, but he tells me he takes a lot of kidding from them. They tell him: you've got to be joking about the police test! (16)

All the respondents believe that test standards have been simplified or modified so that the police department can recruit more black and Puerto Rican policemen. Thus a major source of personal pride has been devalued, and this devaluation is expressed by speaking of "decline in standards":

> Today, to get more blacks on, they have relaxed the standards —not relaxed, they have lowered the barriers all the way on this, and I honestly don't feel that is right. No one did anything

for anybody at any other time to have them get the job insofar
as relaxing the barriers to let them in. And we always had a
decent police force. But today they have become so idealistic
that we have to give this fellow a chance because he has been
held down. . . . It's no favor to him. It's no favor to the Department. And it certainly is no favor to the people of the city.
And I think it's wrong and they have no business doing this. (28)

The alleged decline in standards evokes strong and even passion-
ate beliefs, and a feeling of injustice and bitterness is the result:

It's terribly unfair to ask me to pay for past injustices against
blacks, as no doubt there were and as no doubt there will be in
the future. . . . And it gets kind of annoying after awhile to get
this minority thing thrown in your face and used to rip out a
job that you honestly felt pride and satisfaction. They are tearing this job apart with this minority business today. I say: keep
the department free of politics. Don't use this job as a proving
ground for their new experiments on race relations. Go back to
civil service standards. (28)

We have to let deprived people on the job, they tell us, because
they didn't have the same opportunities. . . . And because of
politics they are letting in the dregs of humanity in my opinion.
And they are going in there and saying because they were
deprived we have to make it easier for them on the tests. That
wasn't my fault that they were deprived. I had nothing to do
with that because they were deprived. (26)

Minority recruitment is a problem for the department. Media campaigns to attract blacks and Puerto Ricans into the ranks of the
police, using television and radio announcements, civil service bul-
letins and programs, posters, and advertising in black and Hispanic
newspapers and magazines have been a dismal failure.[3] Moreover,
blacks with the qualifications to become policemen can now easily
find better-paying opportunities.

A shortage of black captains and of blacks in other high-ranking
positions is also felt by the department. Not enough blacks have

been able to pass the required civil service examinations, and the pool from which candidates were drawn for appointment was much too small. Thus, those who form policy believe they must find new ways to attract blacks.[4]

A special effort in this direction was the establishment of the Model Cities Program, which was designed in 1966 to attack inadequate and substandard housing, unemployment, and education in ghetto neighborhoods, and to involve community residents in direct planning of methods to improve city services such as sanitation and health. In dispute, among our police, is the program that trains young Harlem, South Bronx, and Central Brooklyn residents to take a special Police Department entrance exam so that they can serve in these same neighborhoods. Attempts to devise a special exam that would be "fair" to these residents and help recruit blacks is equated by one police officer with a decline in standards and the overall quality of the job:

> When I see what is coming on today, not only stories, but I've got a copy of the final examination for this new Model Cities Police Cadet Program. And the questions are unbelievable. . . . Now I was told after reading this exam, and I believe it, that the study material for this Model Cities Program was third grade English and they sent the material back to the planning bureau and they said the guys taking the exam could not comprehend the third grade English, and they had to lower the reading ability. . . . And in six and a half years that I've been on the Police Department this job has gone straight downhill. It is not going downhill, it has taken a plunge! (37)

The policemen contend that they are interested in pursuing the ideal of merit; they believe the department is more interested in the public relations advantages of advancing minorities into the force than in merit.

Policemen also feel that to have a certain number of jobs provided for blacks because of race rather than because of individual qualifications creates a double standard, which is a form of discrimination against whites:

I would say they are using different standards for this black group and a different standard for whites. And what do you have? Well, you have the basis for prejudice right away. This guy got on the job because he is this or that. (31)

Another policeman is even more shrill in his criticism of a double standard:

Now I don't hold any bias or prejudice against anybody if a man can take the test and pass it and become a police officer. If a man can qualify under the same test that I had to qualify under, fine. That makes him a good citizen of good character. But don't turn around and use that double standard which they say we use on the street on us! . . . This is the real double standard. They are going to take a man who is an outsider to us. . . . He is not a peer by any sense of the word. The man's educational background, the man's moral background, his character and everything. He just doesn't fit the suit. And if you don't fit the suit you can't wear it. (20)

The attempt to alter or lower the qualifying scores when too few blacks have passed examinations is seen as preferential treatment that gives a competitive advantage to blacks over white candidates. It is also felt to undermine or undercut the achievements of whites:

I could tell you that in the Academy I worked my butt off. Because of my less education I have always felt that I have to put that much more out; I have to work that much harder. I had an 85 average academically which I was very proud of but there were some blacks who didn't make it academically, yet they were passsed anyway. And that's wrong! (19)

However, one police officer suggests that standards are precisely what the tests lack, since they do not show or test an applicant's abilities as a policeman, or very much else that is relevant, for that matter:

I don't know what they actually want. They seem to stress

arithmetic. I use that word instead of mathematics or calculus. They stress vocabulary words, English grammar; I mean like adjectives or dangling participles. This is what they ask you on the test. It is a sentence test. What bearing does this have on whether you are qualified or not? What kind of a test is that? That's no test. It shows you can speak English. . . . I don't think they want to test you. They want to say that you have taken a test. They don't really want to test to see what your potential is. (31)

Blacks would probably agree with this observation. But they would argue that the tests are inherently discriminatory since blacks are apt to have less experience in situations requiring verbal and test-taking skills.[5] White policemen often refer to the rejection of so many blacks through civil service tests as proof that very few blacks are qualified to enter their ranks. In a similar fashion, white policemen are critical of the special exam given to Model Cities cadets because they support strict enforcement of civil service standards, but black neighborhood office workers believe such standards serve to exclude from jobs the very people Model Cities is designed to help.

Another example that standards have been lowered is offered in this estimate by a respondent of the native intelligence of his colleagues. He states that recent candidates for police work do not have the intellectual level that will enable them to function in the same settings and with the same degree of professional skill as their counterparts who came into the department under a more rigorous process of selection:

Yes, it is a very sore spot for policemen with time on the job. Definitely, the standard has been lowered. The average IQ for patrolman at the time that I came on was better than 100. A 107 or 110 was the average IQ. This is not so today. I believe that the IQ is down to 85. These people would have a hard time doing this job. They couldn't understand the concepts of this job, of what to do. They don't think fast enough. This is a job where you have to think. Not everyone who goes out there can play cop. (15)

Another policeman is more direct in telling us who "these people"
are:

I'll give you an example of what is going on here: the class
of 1968 was a special group. The average IQ of this group went
down to 70. And they were all minorities. That is, they did a
survey of this group where they found that the IQ was lower
than the accepted minimum to get into the Police Department.
And they found that seventy percent of them were already in
serious trouble in the department. You can't motivate morons!
(36)[6]

Thus, our respondents believe that the department is failing to
find out through its test procedures which candidates are acceptable
and which are not and what performance variables are, in fact,
measured by standardized tests. It has also failed to eliminate men
who are physically and mentally unfit for appointment to police
work.

But it is not the decline in physical requirements, nor the lack
of intelligence or ability to pass written tests that is the most galling
for our policemen; it is the failure of the Police Department to
weed out those candidates who are considered to be socially and
morally unfit to wear the police uniform.

THE DECLINE IN CHARACTER AND MORAL STANDARDS.   The most acri-
monious controversy concerning the "decline in standards" is the
belief that the Police Department no longer refuses to hire candidates with a criminal record. Our respondents view this as an abro-
gation of civil service rules and regulations, which forbids hiring
candidates with records of criminal acts and associations.[7]

Forty policemen contend that the background investigation inquir-
ing into an applicant's arrest records has either been completely
abandoned or is conducted after the appointment.[8] This means that
many policemen who are on street and radio patrol duty entering
homes and places of business have never been checked for criminal
records.

In the past a man was first investigated and only after he was investigated was a decision made as to whether he should be appointed to the Police Department. Today a decision is made to appoint the man and *then* to investigate him, or at least to complete the investigation. As a result of this, we have guys in the department who have been arrested while they were in uniform, and on post, by authorities who have wanted these men in other states. (13)

Moreover, the department appoints men who have been convicted of at least one misdemeanor. And many of these convictions they feel were felonies at the time of commission and arrest. Allegedly, what happens is this. To have his sentence reduced to a lesser charge, the defendant "sells" his guilty plea in a game called "plea bargaining," which involves the defense counsel, assistant district attorney, and judge. Plea bargaining or "copping pleas" has become part of our court system because the state does not have the time nor money to afford the defendant the luxury of presumed innocence by jury trial. Thus some of our law enforcement agents are convicted felons.

Years ago the standards for the job was that no one could take on the job if he was convicted for any type of crime. Of course, this doesn't include traffic violations and crimes of that sort. Then what happened? They couldn't get enough applicants. So they were taking anyone who was commited for a murder! Now here is what I am getting after. If you are arrested for a felony you can cop a plea for a misdemeanor. Now here is a man let us say who has broken the law to the fullest extent. He has committed a felony. And because of our court system you can plea a lesser charge. . . . This means that he is eligible to take a cop's test because the Police Department will accept people who have been charged with misdemeanors. (6)

This change in standards is seen as affecting all policemen: the department is allowing men on the job with criminal records and this degrades the job.[9]

Since I've been on the job, as far as criminal records go, this is one of the biggest changes and I am very, very strongly opposed to it. . . . Some guys today who are getting on the job who were arrested for, maybe, an armed robbery. This is happening. This is not a myth. (27)

Definitely, it's true! I have heard stories about this black cop who came on the job who had been arrested for a felony and had been convicted but he was given like a suspended sentence. This definitely downgrades the job. (19)

Many policemen take "potshots" at the Preventive Enforcement Patrol Squad (PEP) as evidence for the decline in character standards. The PEP squad was founded and assembled in Harlem in 1969 by a high-ranking black police officer. Its purpose was to patrol the five-precinct area north of Fifty-Ninth Street and to cut down on policy makers, narcotics peddlers, and muggers. The twenty black and Puerto Rican volunteers were all high school dropouts who had completed police cadet school. All of them had grown up in ghetto areas. Many had minor police records.

It is clear from the following account that these men are seen as endangering the prestige of the police and are thereby a cause for mortification.

Some people in the community if they knew there were guys on the job with yellow sheets [arrest records] they would be mortified. Really! I'll give you an example: Myself and my partner. My partner is a Negro. We were riding in a radio car and we had a guy come up to us, and he was a junky, and he says: "You know this guy around the corner, he makin' like he's a cop." So we go check on this guy and this "cop" is on the PEP squad. And this junky tells us how can this guy be a cop: "Man, he took a fall like me for robbery." Which means he was locked up for robbery, right? And then it may have been thrown out of court for a misdemeanor. How did he get on the job? And here was a junky, and he said: "Man, I think I take the test." As a police officer, myself and my partner, being very honest about it, it turned my stomach! And I would be lying

if I said otherwise. I wanted to go out and beat the Jesus out of
this guy on the gall of thinking of being a policeman. . . . (27)

Those on the PEP squad are viewed as marginal cops with no
fixed legal police status; they are possible troublemakers, addicts,
and felons.

We have guys coming in on the job who are convicted criminals,
convicted felons. The PEP squad is made up entirely of this
type of criminal. They are all convicted criminals, and this is
the requirement to get into the police department. . . . These
clucks think you get a shield to steal. Now I am talking about
thirty or forty percent of the guys coming in. Now the administration wants this type of guy—to get more votes from minority
groups, and to undermine the police. (13)

Other policemen resort to a kind of irony or gallows humor to
modulate their bitterness at what they consider to be a department
scandal:

They feel they are good thieves to begin with and therefore
they can catch thieves better. All the signs say "New York's
Finest." And we are letting in the worst. (12)

Of course we are told through the grapevine that these men
can relate more to the community. You have the PEP squad up
in Harlem. Most of these men were trained and lived in this
particular area all their lives, therefore, they can relate
more. . . . It seems today that a qualification for advancement
is a previous narcotics arrest, and that this somehow makes you
a better cop. You are more aware of the problem if you were
on it yourself. (10)

Yet despite this resentment and anger over the policy of hiring
men with arrest records, it is clear from a recent, though not con-
clusive, study of the Rand Institute that a candidate's arrest history
(not involving violent crimes) prior to being appointed to the
department does not adversely affect his police performance. On

the contrary, the study found that he is "less likely than other officers to be later charged with false arrest, illegal search and seizure," and "detaining a person without cause."[10] Apparently, the Rand people believe that if a man has been convicted of a crime, this personal experience will moderate his relations with crime suspects.

THE BEHAVIOR OF MODEL CITIES CADETS IN THE POLICE ACADEMY.   A special aspect of police bitterness toward the decline in moral standards is illustrated by the behavior of Model Cities cadets in the Police Academy. Our respondents speak of spontaneous and mindless acts of destruction; stealing of guns, typewriters, uniforms, and other personal and institutional property; muggings; academy walls marred with graffiti; profanity; insubordination; methodone addiction; indifference toward personal grooming standards; and a general expression of contempt for everything and everybody.[11]

What the policemen regard as pointless malice, which they believe has made life in the academy unpleasant, may simply illustrate that the enemy has now entered the gates.

At the Police Academy now there are characters—you have to understand that they have taken the lowest dregs of Harlem. . . . There is much better kids than this in Harlem. I know this! I was there. These kids in the Police Academy are nodding. And everybody just turns their head and says this is the system and this is how it works. Anybody who knows a junky can see these guys are junkies. I've seen two of them in the hall, it's unbelievable—boxing, knocking things over, cops' guns being locked in the lockers, thirty odd typewriters stolen in the Police Academy. They are stealing! It's unbelievable. We are in the Police Academy and have security. We have lockers and we are not allowed to leave our guns in the academy. Can you believe it? We have to take our guns home overnight. Hey, what's hapening? The people have to know about these things. (35)

The same respondent goes on to say:

The Model Cities Program rationalizes this thing. It says we need federal funds and we have to take the good with the bad. Uncle Sam won't give us money unless we take these people on. They tell us that they are not going to be police officers. They are going to be Community Service Officers or something like that. Now this is fine if you go into that community and get the best they have and really educate them and screen them a little. There wasn't any screening. I think they went through Harlem with a net and in a corner got a bunch of kids and this is the way it looks to me. And to hear them talk, the language they use. And you say, well, we are in trouble. (35)

Other policemen report that such affairs as mindless acts of violence and wanton vandalism are common:

In the academy they mugged people in full uniform. What do you think of that? Not only that, they wrote four letter words on the academy walls. They were tearing it down. They tore tiles off the wall. They were very destructive. (1)

Policemen also express resentment against the accommodations that cadets receive (in spite of this behavior) at the expense of regular patrolman.

And now probationary officers [regular patrolmen] have to use basement lockers which are little two-by-four lockers. . . . Meanwhile these people [cadets] are getting big lockers and can hang their stuff in it because they need more space and yet they stick this probationary guy down in the basement. . . . (14)

There is also a very explicit tradition concerning the dress of police officers, and regulations that require uniform standards of dress while in the academy. Any deviation from such standards is recognized as contempt for order, propriety, and for the values of authority and respectability.[12] Hence slovenly dress on the part of cadets shows not only disrespect for the occasion but for police officers who consider the uniform to be a symbol of prestige and honor:[13]

Take for example their hair. Their hair is not supposed to be long, it should be in contour with your head. . . . Their hat is sittin' a foot above their head. Again, you have to wear black socks, and I have seen many with white socks or brown shoes when you have to wear black shoes. (22)

You see them walking with their collars open, their hats in the back of their heads. Some people would say they look sloppy, but I know it is contempt. . . . They know what the regulations are on how to wear a uniform. (35)

Even such a seemingly trivial matter as using the gym floor when it is prohibited is seen as insubordination:

In the gym you are not allowed to use the basketball at certain times. But while they are in the gym they are always playing ball. They were told not to but they played anyhow. . . . But they are more lenient with these people because they are black. (22)

It should be clear that the preceding discussion of the decline in standards is related to the wider problem of integration of blacks into police ranks. Can whites work together with blacks in new areas of opportunity? The solution of the white policeman is to create white enclaves to monopolize opportunities. If successful, this tactic would lead to a bureaucratic reinforcement of the caste system in the department. But if this is not to happen some other solution, one based on genuine integration, must be found. To overcome the institutional disabilities of blacks through integration, opportunities must be created for blacks and whites to work together with the same degree of amicable social relations. Areas of equal opportunity must be provided and sufficient training and skills must be provided to allow blacks to move to all levels of opportunity. A bogus integration means recruiting blacks to positions for which they do not have the skills or meet the requirements, and then condescending to blacks because they lack the skills and fail to meet the requirements.

WHITE POLICEMEN ARE AN EXCEPTION TO THE DECLINE IN STANDARDS. Virtually every policeman who claims that standards have declined regards himself to be the sole exception. In an effort to defend his status, despite the decline in standards, he discovers the superiority of his physical strength, morality, pride, and honor. The following statement from a man who joined the department in 1947 is typical for those who have time on the job.

When I came into the department 50,000 men took the exam for only 2000 positions. I recall the New York *News* saying that you had to be a Tarzan to pass the six component parts of the physical requirements. I'll just give you an example. You had to be able to lift without jerking in a standing position bending down eighty pounds with your right hand, and then pressing up eighty pounds with your left hand. That was only one of the components. To give you an idea of the investigation that was conducted on you, the U.S. consulate where I was born [in Europe] sent investigators to my home town to find out about my parents. To find out if my parents had a record, what type of people they were. The mayor of this town was asked about me. And that was how strict they were at that time. And that was the type of men they wanted in the Police Department. (24)

The following quotations are typical for those who joined the department in 1955. All of these respondents express the desire to build up their egos and repair the damage to their tarnished prestige by making themselves exceptions to the decline in standards.

When the old-timers came in they had to study eleven months. I studied this long. I was investigated. I remember the sergeant when he came around my neighborhood asking people about me, whether I was a good fellow or not. He asked the merchants about me. I remember a man who was denied entrance into the department because his father was a criminal. (17)

When I came on this job there was no relaxing of standards. The fellow I grew up with had a court-martial in the Army because he had been AWOL for two days. Yet he was turned

down by this job. He was considered unfit. Now *he* was a white
Irish Catholic. (28)

Even policemen who joined the department in the late sixties and
have been admitted into police work because of the decline in
standards are likely to go to an extreme in glorifying the entry standards when they entered the department.

I had a little problem in my investigation. I had a couple of
parking summonses that weren't paid and I had a big hassle
about it. . . . It really scared me. It scared the life out of me!
It almost cost me the job. And my promotion was held up
because of it. (37)

I was in an automobile accident, I believe in 1959 in Detroit.
And here it is about 1967 when I joined and this sergeant wants
copies of my hospital record from this hospital in Michigan
where I had my head sewn up. . . . And I wondered why I had
to go through all of this when other guys were getting on who
had been arrested. (34)

I remember when I was going through my investigation he
[the sergeant] was giving me a lot of static because I played
hooky from high school. Now how can you compare this with
a guy who has been convicted of a crime? (18)

It may well be that the standards of a job go up in relation to
the need for prestige. This means that it is much better to have
a job that requires candidates to meet some standards than a job
that accepts misfits or criminals. The white policeman feels better
about himself and his work when he believes or imagines higher
police standards for himself. It is, of course, true that the defense
against social change expressed in the above statements is the conviction of rightness about the white policeman's position. Defending
standards is justified by sacred tradition as well as on the basis of
the social gains whites believe they have made and the necessity to
defend them.

THE PUSH FOR EDUCATION. The need to professionalize and upgrade
the educational level of the police force to improve performance
and attitudes, to subvert prejudices, and to escape the insularity of
the civil service mentality is influencing police departments throughout the country.[14]

Respondents support the department's attempts to raise educational
standards after entry, since a measure of prestige is provided by
work toward a degree.

But continued schooling leads to other problems, for the degree
becomes a compensation for the lack of police work prestige. Certainly the degree becomes a means by which policemen can escape
the boredom and paramilitary discipline of police work and get
another job.

> I know that if I finished college, and if I had my bachelor's
> degree, I would leave this job tomorrow and swing twenty to
> twenty-five thousand dollars. (37)

> If I graduated from college why should I be a policeman in
> uniform and especially nowadays, a target of abuse? You can't
> do a damn thing right. I could be an FBI agent. Much more
> interesting job. I could be a narcotics man. And much more
> interesting than police. I could be a customs man. Very interest-
> ing. In other words, you wouldn't have to worry about whether
> you have your hat on, or whether you are smoking and you are
> not supposed to be smoking. (30)

Yet there are more significant problems facing the police administration. For example, how is the administration going to convince
police officers that they are going to professionalize the job by
raising educational requirements, and then integrate underqualified
men into the department? Most policemen are aware of this contradiction.

> Of course, it has become a joke in the department. A college
> degree if you're white. A yellow sheet [an arrest record] if
> you're black. And it's unfair that they have done this. (28)

Murphy's come out with the statement that you will have to have
one year of college to come on, two years to get promoted to
sergeant, and three years for lieutenant and above. And everybody says, what in the hell are they doing letting these guys
in and making *us* go to college? (36)

Bitterness about this double standard is clear in the answer of
another police officer.

This is definitely a contradiction. It is an inconsistency and
makes me pretty upset. I went through three years of college. I
am a senior now. Now the department comes out and says they
want professionals. But on the other hand they try to lower the
standards. But they aren't trying to lower the standards for
my kind of people. I hate to sound prejudiced but this job
makes you prejudiced. They are lowering the standards for this
group, they are helping the poor, which is fine. But they are
not making it easier for me. And I think they are taking the
first step towards being prejudiced because nobody is giving me
any breaks. They are giving it to them. And these people we
associate with crime. We do associate them with most of our
problems. And it rubs you a little raw to see them getting the
breaks and what are you getting? You're getting the ax. You
get nothing for it. Nothing! (38)

A college degree does not necessarily make a policeman a better
policeman. Doggedness in investigative work, ability to size up a
situation, tolerance under pressure, motivation, aptitude in dealing
with problems involving people, and personal and emotional ad-
justment are all important requisites for police success and may not
be related to education.

I haven't met one man, college degree or not, that doesn't believe
that you need street experience. The policeman needs primarily
an enormous amount of common sense. And a certain amount
of determination to get the job done. An educated police officer
is probably a more patient man. He is probably more understanding of problems, especially race relations. Education is

important. But the basic job of the cop is gutty work, it's a
bloody job. It's downright putrid, you know. And it takes a man.
No job will demand more of your existence. . . . Your courage
is taxed to the fullest the moment you face that gun. Your mental
agility to make decisions and to think things out quickly. Your
physical aspect in running up and down buildings. . . . Now, is
education required to be a good cop? The answer is no. (35)

Other policemen question the value of an education because they
argue that it interferes with immediate summary police action, much
of which is based on instinct or reflex.

One thing that happens is that a better educated guy thinks too
much. (He thinks too much?) Yeah. And if you think too much
you've got a problem. If a guy is running away you are thinking,
can I shoot this guy or not? What can I do? What does it state
in the Rules and Procedures Manual? By this time the guy has
run away. Now, most cops use common sense and won't indis-
criminately shoot people. So I believe that education will interfere with quick responses. Many cops have disciplined their
bodies to the point that they can instinctively react to a situation and they don't think about it. There is really no script for
instinct reaction to a situation. When they give you a script
then it interferes. . . . (36)

Related to this problem is the argument that the policeman
should reflect, as much as possible, the community he serves, and
New York City is not a homogenous community of educated people.
So education for a police officer is considered a relative need.

Well, somebody said quite recently that a policeman is as good
as the society he serves. Now I think what society wants in a
police officer will determine how much education he might need.
Now I've worked in Riverdale. . . . The people up their expect
a bit more from you as far as things like grammar, diction,
common English usage. . . . And you have to speak to these
people in an [educated] manner. But when I worked down in
Brooklyn [in Bedford Stuyvesant] they don't expect you to act

like that. They expect you to solve the problems in any way that they accept as being solved. If you walk into a family fight in Brooklyn and the wife is screaming at you, and the husband is screaming at you, and they are all telling you to have inter- course with your mother . . . if you jack the husband [hit him with a blackjack] everybody is satisfied. . . . This is what they want. . . . But you just can't jack Hymie Schwartz as you did Rufus, you know. It just doesn't work. (38)

In general, then, we may conclude that the repeated references to a decline in standards reflect the feeling that the integration of blacks and Puerto Ricans into police ranks threatens the virtual monopoly and cloistered autonomy of the white policeman's job. In the struggle to control that job, the white policeman plays the politics of prestige and ethnic superiority to freeze out blacks. This in turn allows the white policeman to capture some prestige for himself.

In poverty programs and other civil service jobs the same prob- lems emerge. In poverty programs blacks tend to squeeze out pov- erty officials as agents of the establishment. A central problem of a similar nature is discrimination against Puerto Ricans by blacks. Lack of opportunity in the past clearly results in attempts to monopolize present opportunities. This framework defines the na- ture of police resentment and the loss of self-esteem.

The decline in standards also reflects the racial prejudices of older policemen who complain that the influx of blacks and Puerto Ricans contaminates the force through race mixing, which results in the inevitable decline in standards regardless of the personal attributes of the newer policemen.

In part the decline in standards reflects an overall hostility to the Police Department administration and former Mayor John V. Lindsay, as we see in succeeding chapters. A vast number of police- men have intense hatred for Lindsay and most of his appointees to the police administration. Everything that the Lindsay Administra- tion did with respect to the department seems to evoke negative criticism and comment. The decline in standards is cited as just another tainted legacy of that administration.

The Lindsay Administration supported the aspirations of blacks in community control of education, poverty programs, and civilian review boards of police activity. Lindsay is seen as the man who hampered the Police Department in dealing with the lawlessness of blacks, and who attempted to recruit black policemen and paraprofessionals. These new policemen are an anathema to the older policemen who view themselves as ethnically superior to the population that they feel breeds lawlessness and disorder. Now the enemy has entered the gates, and policemen must deal with them not as offenders but as peers.

NOTES

1. See "Los Angeles Police Recruitment Is Short of Goal," *The New York Times*, September 6, 1967.

2. As reported by Jon Nordheimer, "The Force That Is Always Whiter Than White," *The New York Times*, February 13, 1972.

3. Suggested by the Commanding Officer of the Personnel Research Unit of the New York City Police Department (in correspondence). This was, of course, the case as far back as 1968. See, for example, Robert Terrel, "White Police Bar Negro Cops, RFK Told," *The New York Post*, February 7, 1968.

4. See, for example, Isaac S. Hunt, Jr., and Bernard Cohen, *Minority Recruiting in the New York City Police Department. Part I. The Attraction of Candidates. Part II. The Retention of Candidates*, R-702-NYC, The New York City–Rand Institute, May 1971.

5. Reported by David Burnham, "Suit Calls Police Tests Biased Against Minority Candidates," *The New York Times*, March 4, 1972. Richard Margolis has considered this problem in his excellent article, "Minority Hiring and the Police," *The New Leader*, Vol. 54, No. 16 (August 9, 1971), pp. 13–16.

6. There is some objective evidence to support these observations. According to a report paid for by a Federal grant to the New York City Police Department, the average IQ score for all classes of recruits that entered in 1969 was 98.2. Also, according to the report, two of the recruits who entered the department in July 1968 scored between 70 and 79. In contrast, the IQs of the entering classes for 1964, 1965, 1966, and 1967 ranged from 102.88 to 111.71. But it was also made clear from the findings of the report that the decline of IQ was not related to the city's efforts to recruit more minorities into the department; there were no significant differences in IQ on a racial and ethnic basis, and few blacks and Puerto Ricans had been recruited. As reported by David Burnham, "Walinsky Lays a Serious Decline in Police Quality to Mayor," *The New York Times*, September 7, 1970.

7. For a provocative discussion on the decline in police standards from a retired police lieutenant, see Herbert Klein, "A Policeman (Anon.) Speaks Up," *National Review*, May 6, 1969. For a reprint of this article and extended commentary see *Law Enforcement Group of New York, Inc. Bulletin*, Vol 1, No. 2 (July 1969).

8. The civil service commission traditionally investigated all candidates who applied for jobs as patrolmen before their names were actually certified on the police list. This investigation included a verification of the truthfulness of statements made by the prospective candidate on a civil service application form, such as date and place of birth, previous schooling, history of employment, and present residence. Once the name was certified the applicant was subject to a complete background investigation or check by a sergeant, under the direction of a lieutenant who was especially assigned and trained to that duty. A criminal record automatically disqualified a person for appointment. As reported in the *Law Enforcement Group of New York, Inc. Bulletin*, Vol. 1, No. 2 (July 1969).

9. For a nice example of resistance to this policy from a police commissioner see "Police in Houston Defiant on Hiring," *The New York Times*, January 1, 1975.

10. See Bernard Cohen and Jan M. Chaiken, *Police Background Characteristics and Performance*, R-999-DOJ, The New York City–Rand Institute, August 1972, pp. 87–88.

11. For other problems at the Police Academy not reported on in these interviews see, for example, James M. Markham, "John Jay College Stirred by Charge It Harbors Gamblers," *The New York Times*, January 1, 1972.

12. For a fine historical treatment of uniform standards and their social functions for New York City police see James F. Richardson, *The New York Police: Colonial Times to 1901* (New York: Oxford University Press, 1970), pp. 46, 48, 64 66, 90, 120.

13. See Nathan Joseph and Nicholas Alex, "The Uniform: A Sociological Perspective," *American Journal of Sociology*, Vol. 77, No. 4 (January 1972). On the multifaceted meanings given to the uniform by police officers see David Burnham, "Police Upbraided on Their Grooming," *The New York Times*, November 13, 1972.

14. See Lacey Fosburgh, "College Training Is Goal of Police," *The New York Times*, September 28, 1971, and Robert D. McFadden, "Police End Limit On Study Leaves," *The New York Times*, October 16, 1971.

3

The Opposition of White Policemen to Changing Work Styles

To the extent that we were able to find a positive image of police work it was of the policeman as a free, independent, active, masculine, autonomous man. In this romantic vision, the policeman is free from the burden of a fixed routine. He can express his self-image and is backed up by the power of his own manhood, of the state, and of his weapon. His self-image suggests a hope for overcoming a sense of alienation, of impersonality, of anonymity, and loss of identity under the pressures and confusions of modern urban life undergoing radical change.

We have indicated to some extent that this image emanates from television, and to a far lesser extent from the image of authority that a policeman on the beat might give to an adolescent.

The reality of police work is far removed from these images. Any urban police department is necessarily a bureaucracy.[1] The policeman is hedged in with a vast number of legal and administrative controls subordinating him to bureaucratic law and to those rules that will enable his commanders to supervise, control, and evaluate him on a regular basis and be able to separate him from the force if he does not measure up. Paper work is central to this system of control.

On paper, the policeman's routine is highly specified. The beat, tours of duties, and forms of making arrests are highly circumscribed by written regulations. The policeman must fill in a vast number of reports and forms on such matters as vehicular accidents, gun permits, pawnshop transactions, stolen property and stolen cars, and traffic summonses. At least in principle, the paper work must be done with sufficient accuracy to allow the roughly 235 commanders who supervise the activity of 31,000 policemen on the street at any given time to know what has happened, why, and how.[2]

Human nature being what it is, there will be deviations from these standards of control due to ignorance. There will be delays in handling over reports and disagreements over their contents due to rigid adherence to perfectly genuine, but incompatible views of police officers and their commanders. This is why planning, discipline, leadership, and above all constant supervision are necessary if the police bureaucracy is to operate effectively.[3]

More importantly, these reports, while they may be onerous in themselves, serve to make policemen accountable to their superiors and to the civilians who allegedly control the Police Department. Several significant characteristics of police work prompt this type of control.

First, as in the army, the policeman has at his command the legitimate use of violence. He has the right to shoot if necessary and to use physical violence on a law violater. Even the military does not exercise powers as continuously and directly as the policeman, in part because in most countries the military operates against an external enemy, and partly because wars are intermittent. Hence the policeman is a special figure in government because he has the power to decide what is reasonable enforcement of the laws.[4]

Second, the person on whom violence is practiced is in principle innocent until proven guilty, and therefore has political recourse against policemen to the extent to which he may, like any other citizen, be politically effective. But in addition, the very nature of the amount of power that a policeman can bring to bear in direct social relations provides opportunities for bribery, graft, corruption, as well as terrorism, personal brutality, racial animosity, and the acting out of resentments against the powerless and vulnerable because of his own personal feeling of low esteem or prestige and lack of power.[5]

When evidence of abuse of police power occurs, therefore, the Police Department must control, investigate, and punish the policeman who violates manifest duties and regulations. But such control entails surveillance, and surveillance means investigations and paper work that devalue the idealized image of the policeman as a free, untrammeled, personal actor who can determine the character of his work and the manner in which it is performed.

What are the attitudes and psychological reactions of policemen to these bureaucratic controls? In particular, to what extent are these reactions related to changes in work styles and to changes in the composition of the force as this is expressed in strict enforcement of rules of procedure? When we look at these controls we see that they produce in policemen an attitude of deep dissatisfaction and grievance, primarily because they must now divest themselves of almost everything they expected or believed about the job.

PAPER WORK DEBASES THE POLICE IMAGE. Policemen can muster great indignation over the flow of paper work they are required to handle in the course of a day. In fact, all of the interviews (except for those with two high-ranking officers) can be read from beginning to end without finding a single note of enthusiasm for the volume of paper work. An example from a patrolman who works in the Youth Aid Division:

> It's a Mickey Mouse outfit. In the military you called it "chicken shit." I have never seen it to become as bad as it has become in the last six months. It is so bad that you are literally bogged down with reams and reams of paper work. An arrest report is unbelievable. And yet we are the greatest believers of carbon paper. We will make six or seven reports requiring carbon paper. A narcotics arrest requires the preparation of fourteen different forms. And each form has four or five carbon sheets with it. (26)

As a result, policemen are angry that they are not free to do what they consider real police work—prevention of crime and detection and apprehension of criminals.

I would like to go out there and work, but you really can't. Specifically, in narcotics there is so much paper work. I have four partners and for the most part we work together or we break into a three-man team or a two-man team. But we never work alone, so there is at least two of us. And at the end of the day we have to put in a form called a Daily Activity Report. I have to put in one. My partner has to put in one. If the five of us work together we have to submit five individual forms, each with the same report. Now, that's a triplicate copy, or a minimum of fifteen sheets of the same words for each man, or a total of seventy-five sheets! . . . And it slows you down and really prevents you from doing investigative work. In other words, I spend more time filling out forms and very little time actually doing the work I have been trained to do. (34)

Complaints are also expressed by a uniformed patrolman:

Like I say, there is no job satisfaction anymore in the Police Department. When I first came on the job [1957] the paper work was already at an all-time high for the guys who were already in, and the paper work has been constantly building. Now since I've come on, the paper work is getting massive. . . . And this keeps so many men involved in clerical work that could have been out on patrol and concerned with street crimes. (33)

These policemen are not simply complaining about the sheer volume of paper work they must handle, nor that paper work prevents them from taking an active part in what they consider to be good police work. They are also complaining about the *level of work* required to carry out pencil and paper tasks. In other words, they feel that filling out forms and reports prevents them from fully utilizing their skills, abilities, and training. In this sense, policemen feel they are underemployed, since their paper tasks require low skill requirements.

Moreover, the psychology of the policeman is undermined at its most vital point, the impulse to react instinctively, to express himself in highly personal terms by determining how and when to be aggressive. Paper work deprives him of the positive satisfaction potentially inherent in his work by making him accountable for all his actions. Yet this is the very reason why the Police Department finds it necessary to control police behavior in even simple tasks.

Today you are a secretary. A secretary riding around with a gun on your belt. In a precinct like I am in where we take in reports more than anything else in great quantity, I can be busy over the phone for five or six hours every day just handling stolen car reports or past burglaries instead of being out trying to catch a perpetrator. (25)

When I came on the job you were able to hold court on the street; you were the judge. You could give a guy a rap over the head and that was the end of it right there. . . . I think one of the saddest things on this job is to see a cop who really enjoyed being a cop. He comes on the job and is all fired up with it. He really enjoys the work he is doing and suddenly he runs into the first case and they tell him you can't do that because of regulations. The man telling him he can't do it knows the cop is right. But under present policies we can't do it. The disillusionment starts and then after several years of it you don't have a good hard charging cop giving good police service to the people. You have a cynic on your hands. (28)

We turn now to examine the psychological responses of policemen to other types of mechanical and visual controls used by the department to bring about improved levels of police performance by trying to eliminate "beating time" (cooping), inefficiency on duty (loafing), and police misconduct.

THE SCRATCH: SYMBOLIC RITE OF CLOSE SUPERVISION. A book is supplied to all policemen for the purpose of recording, in a precise and compact manner, his whereabouts during his tour of duty. This memo book is a form of working time table which logs, and preserves the meaning of, the time, assignment, location, and disposition of events and activities while on patrol. In addition, this book must be signed or verified by a field commander ("shoo-fly") when the patrolman is out on post or walking a beat, or by a sergeant in the station house when the patrolman begins his tour of duty, and when he goes off duty. The signing or corroboration of this memo book is referred to as a "scratch."

The "scratch" has practical application and is of value to supervisors in determining whether a policeman is in fact out on post. By checking the entries in the book, the supervisor gets some idea of whether patrol time is being wasted. Thus it allows supervisors to control and direct patrol time, makes policemen accountable, and fixes responsibility. All police officers are required to keep their memo books for several years.

But there is the human problem of psychological reactions to the use or abuse of this form of control. The following officer complains that the surfeit of "scratches" repeatedly exacted by superiors is a form of oversupervision.

> Well, the job has changed tremendously. It was a lot more easy going when I came on. In other words, nobody was on your back all the time. . . . Now when I first came on the job you would go out on post and you would be out maybe an hour or an hour and a half and you would get your scratch. And you wouldn't see the boss for the rest of the night. Now, it's not uncommon to get three or four scratches a night. They are out there looking for you. And it's a form of harassment. (38)

The "scatch" allows the supervisor to direct and evaluate policemen on a regular basis. But our respondents feel that this means of control has become an end in itself when supervisors overemphasize the intrinsic value of it. To them, nothing is more destructive of initiative and morale than excess supervision from above which appears unreasonable, arbitrary, and capricious.

> Before where I worked we never even saw a shoo-fly [field

supervisor] because of where we worked. It wasn't because we
didn't do our job. The thing was that if you worked in a busy
house, they never bothered you generally. They would pop in
and check if you signed out. Now they are there constantly.
Almost every day or at least every other day. Just constantly
checking on you. They are making sure that we come in at four
o'clock and that at the end of the tour you have signed out.
That you sign your name out and you don't sign somebody
else's. . . . This is supervision? This is what they used to do
in 1930 but they are still doing it now. It's a picayune and
penny-ante kind of supervision. (30)

Moreover, police reactions to the arbitrary use of supervisory
power are generally negative because it communicates two things:
first, even though their jobs are ostensibly responsible, this type of
supervision treats them as if they were errant schoolboys who should
be punished for their indiscretions, and is therefore incompatible
with the responsibility associated with their positions; second, they
are distrusted by superiors who have no confidence that policemen
have the intention or even the ability to accomplish or carry out
normal and routine police matters.

Such communications or accusations not only agitate policemen,
but also lead to discontent and sagging morale.

We are in the Dark Ages when it comes to supervision or to
the methods we use. . . . The night before last there were fourteen men—I counted about $180,000 worth of police talent from
the borough of Manhattan who had to run over to the 10th
precinct to have their memo books signed by a captain. Some of
the men came from the 26th precinct, some from the 30th precinct which is up in Manhattan, and also from the 2-3 [23rd
precinct]. $200,000 worth of talent, counting the captain who
makes about $26,000 a year, of guys standing around and wait-
ing for a captain who has no more interest in this job than the
man in the moon. . . . And this was the department's way of
saying that the men are supervised. . . . This is a method of
supervision that is a complete waste. It's treating you like
ten-year old children. (26)

But "negative supervision" is also seen as a way of fostering status differences between the superior and the men under his command. Thus arbitrary exactions of supervisory power are considered to be symbols of deference. This leaves the superior free to refuse to discuss certain issues with a patrolman or to ignore the requests of a patrolman who is stepping out of the confines of his deference role. Underlying this is resentment and indignation.

We had to take a copy of a report of an incident involving two Chinese children that were stabbed to death to the captain's house on Staten Island. Now I said to him, "Why can't you hear it over the phone? I am going to read you what is on this paper, on this letterhead." "No," he says, "I want a copy of it in my hands, and that's an order. You bring that letterhead over to Staten Island, to my home there." I say, "Captain: I don't even know where you live in Staten Island, and I don't know the Island." "You'll find it," he says. "Just ask!" There were $26,000 worth of talent in a radio car that had to go over the Verrazano Bridge and mope around to find some silly address there. . . . The attitude that prevails is, what do you have to do for eight hours anyway? But I resent being a messenger boy. I resent being used, relegated to tasks to deliver a thing that could easily have been done over the phone. . . . And I regard this as a fault of the supervisor, not a problem in supervision. . . . So I think we are $13,000 a year of gofers at times. (26)

RINGING IN: THE STIFFENING OF STANDARD OPERATING PROCEDURE. All policemen are required to make hourly rings through the call-box system to the switchboard operator of the precinct station house to which they are assigned.[6] The policeman maybe directed to ring in ten minutes after the hour (ten ring), twelve minutes after the hour (twelve ring), and so on. After 3 P.M. he must make two rings; one ring fifteen minutes after the hour, the second ring at forty-five minutes after the hour. This traditional procedure for foot patrolmen has recently been applied to radio cars as well. Radio car operators no longer have the "luxury" of ringing in from the car

telephone. For plainclothes narcotics undercovermen the procedure
is varied slightly: these men may ring in every two hours from a
public phone booth; presumably to allow them maximum anonymity.
In all cases, when the patrolman rings in he must give his location
and the phone number from which he is calling. If he is in a radio
car, he also identifies the car he is in and gives the name of the partner with whom he is working. In addition, he must ring in when he
goes for a "personal" (that is, to relieve himself), when he goes to
eat, and when he completes his meal.

For the most part, ringing in is a formality. It is part of the social
ritual of rules and regulations that defines the responsibilities of the
patrolman and the authority of the command structure. It is a form
of discipline through which the department is able to consistently
exert control over the actions of the ranks. But this formality is
not one-sided, for it confers an equal benefit to the patrolman. It
serves to protect the patrolman when he needs help. When a policeman does not ring in, the station house quickly sends a radio car
to investigate.

I have no objections at all to making hourly rings. Part of this
is important. Let's put it this way: the other day I had a park
post and I was the only guy in the area where I had a mile and
a half of streets plus the park itself to patrol. I could have
been involved in an accident where I could have been thrown
from the scooter, knocked unconscious, and still be out on the
street someplace. If I didn't make my ring I know the supervisor would be informed of this and immediately radio cars
would be sent out to look for me, to find out where I was and
why I wasn't able to make my ring. This definitely is an asset
on the job. And it should be strictly enforced. (15)

More typical is the complaint that ringing in interferes with the
work rhythms of the police officer; it creates a mechanical pace that
is neither chosen nor variable, but imposed and fixed. It also dis-
tracts his attention from what is happening on the street, and therefore interferes with the police function even when that function may
be inefficient.

Like on my late tour we missed the first ring. We had parked
on Atlantic Avenue and we were watching a place that had
been hit [robbed] a couple of times. The owner was always
screaming so we were watching it. That was about ten after
three in the morning. We stayed about till a quarter to four and
then we drove around and the lieutenant wanted to know why
we didn't ring. You have to ring he says. You weren't on the
job. And they give you all kinds of static. So to hell with the
guy getting hit. You ring and you play it by the book. You play
it like little wooden soldiers. You do exactly like he says. Instead of trying to do something good, you just forget about it.
So when you are curbed for little things you just don't have
the interest anymore. (18)

Dissatisfaction with the police ring stems in part from the problem
of finding a workable call box. The policeman is sometimes late in
his ring and is reprimanded for it by a superior officer because the
department does not accept even valid excuses for a late ring.

Now half the call boxes don't work. They really don't. If one
falls off the hook it knocks over the whole system. And the light
goes on in the switchboard and it stays on constantly so the
switchboard operator puts in a plug and knocks the whole line
out. He's got to do that because if he doesn't the buzzer will just
keep ringing and there's nobody on the line. But then they get
you if you are late for the ring. (18)

An undercover man finds the same problem with nonoperable
public phones:

When I was an undercover we were supposed to make rings
every two hours and we would work in areas where there are
just not any phones on the street, like, parts of Harlem or parts
of Queens, that are working. And then if you call in late they
want to know why you didn't make the ring on time. So if you
don't ring you could end up with some sort of jam with your
boss. (34)

Even when he makes his ring, he may be required to wait for a visual inspection or verification of his location by a superior officer. Some policemen may be dishonest about what they say over the phone, but all policemen feel they are being treated as if they are dishonest.

We are supposed to ring in every two hours to call the office and give them our location, the car you are in—we use our own cars—the partners that you are with, and the phone number that you are at. And whoever answers the phone directs you to wait for a superior to come down. And you have to wait there! . . . And, if for example, we are out on Second Avenue and Fourteenth Street, and there are three of us, and it is time for us to make a ring, one guy will go in to a phone and give the location. And if someone says wait there we are coming down, and the boss gets there and they have him down saying he is with the three of us when he is in fact there by himself, well, we are all in a jam. So they check to make sure you are there. I could conceivably call from here [his apartment] and say I'm there. (34)

Other policemen express anger at the rule because it is not enforced consistently, and this reflects unfavorably upon those who are in command. Moreover, the supervisor who is aware of a failure to ring in, rather than reminding the patrolman of his "memory lapse" may proceed to charge him with a violation of regulations. This may require him to appear at a hearing, and is considered a form of "entrapment" of which policemen are the victims, since it rests primarily on the principle of deception. The method is that of the ambush and snare. Thus policemen are angry not only because they have become victims, but also because they have been outwitted by superior officers.

There is a big crusade to put the job on the level and all hell breaks loose for a period of time. Just recently radio cars in my precinct are supposed to make an hourly ring. But the guys just don't do it. So the switchboard operator writes down that the radio car made the ring. Now by some great detective work [respondent says this sarcastically] on the part of the command they see a radio car parked outside the station house, and they see that the guys have not put in a ring. So they go inside the station house and give the switchboard a complaint because they know the cop did not ring in. And they wouldn't let the radio car ring in after the guys were notified about it. This is not only ridiculous. This is entrapment. (9)

POLICEMEN UNDER SURVEILLANCE. The Police Department has always had some form of internal security by which it tries to control and evaluate itself by professional standards. This policing is presently being carried out by the Inspections Division of the Inspectional Services Bureau, which reports directly to the First Deputy Commissioner, the second-ranking man in the department. Its span of control is far-reaching. It investigates the overall operations of the borough commands, then the divisions, and finally the precincts, the smallest units in the command structure. Its aim is to assure that policemen carry out their professional obligations of serving the public with a certain degree of efficiency. This idea is hardly more radical in civil service than in private enterprise, where a man who does not do his job gets punished, reassigned, demoted, or fired. Internal security is a type of industrial engineering that collects data on police performance and develops methods to measure it for the purpose of directing and improving existing conditions of patrol time. To get maximum return on the costs of radio cars and labor to operate them, one must find ways to maximize patrol time. Thus delays must be analyzed as they effect patrol as well as the loss of time on the part of individual policemen.

The men who carry out this duty are called "field investigators" by the men in the ranks. Like efficiency experts, they make random checks on all precincts to see if a given post is covered (that is, to make sure cops are not "cooping") or if it is up to standard; they check the patrolling pattern of radio cars to and from their respective assignments and locations; they check the frequency with which the precinct sergeant and lieutenant check up on these assigned duties, and hold them accountable if they do not; and they follow up all tips and complaints against policemen regardless of the source. They mostly work in civilian clothes; they travel in unmarked cars; and they seldom announce their visits. Our respondents consider their methods unfair and odious.[7]

You feel they are timing you from the time you get the call and from the time they hang the phone up to the time you get to the location; how you get out of the car; and how you go into the apartment. In all, they time you to see how fast it takes you to get to a particular job. (30)

One police officer complains that the field supervisor or investigator prevents him from doing what he wants:

Well, the difficultly now is that you can't normally do the job like you want to. The supervision is terribly, terribly tight. It is unbearable. For instance: there are assignments given to radio cars and the supervisors follow the cars to their assignments. They follow the radio car to their destination to see how long they take on this job. In other words, you have to watch the clock. Of course, there are men who find a way to kill a lot of time. This is not correct. But everybody is now watching the clock because you know that the supervisor is responding to the same call that you are responding to. And I believe, although I can't prove this, that radio cars are being monitored. This would mean that certain station houses are being tapped. And it's kinda rough to work under these conditions. And the men are not at ease when they work and they lose a lot of initiative because of this close supervision, and checks, and surveillance. In other words, I don't think the supervisors trust the men. (17)

Moreover, they express apprehension about the growing influence that the borough captain (the division commander) has over the power, authority, and autonomy of their precinct commanders. It is apparent from the following quotation that it is the borough captain or commander rather than the captain of the precinct who disciplines men who commit violations of departmental rules and regulations:

> They bring in supervision from outside commands instead of having direct supervision within the commands like the sergeant, lieutenant, and captain. The bosses in the precinct understand more and don't pressure you as much. The pressure always comes from outside the command. The pressure does not come from the precinct. The shoo-fly comes in, who is usually the division captain who is in charge of discipline, that is, catching you from going wrong. And these division captains have to show activity. So they have to make observations, like for instance you get caught smoking. And then they write up an observation. If you get caught with your hat off—you are supposed to wear your hat in the radio car but a lot of guys don't—that's an observation or a complaint. If you get two observations you get a complaint. The complaint is a very serious thing. You have to go before a trial room downtown at headquarters. Being late is a complaint. (18)

However, a procedure called "command discipline," which went into effect in October 1971, gives the local precinct commander sole responsibility for disciplining men in his command.[8] Under this procedure, if a charge is brought against a policeman, let us say by a borough shoo-fly or the captain supervisor of patrol for a borough, the local precinct commander will hear the testimony. If he finds the policeman guilty, he can reprimand him or dock his pay, vacation or holiday time, or take away other benefits, up to a maximum of five days. The severity of the punishment is left to each commander's discretion. It should be noted that command discipline does not involve serious crimes, like criminal charges, which are still handled by the regular court system and trials division—nor the complaints filed by civilians with the Civilian Complaint Review Board. Furthermore, after a year, if the policeman has not committed any other infraction of department rules, his personal record is destroyed, which was not the case under the old system. The policeman can, if he chooses, have a statutory hearing at headquarters, as in the past. But if he chooses this option, the infraction goes on his permanent record whether he "beats" the charge or not. This, of course, discourages policeman from volunteering for departmental trials.

Command discipline is in keeping with Commissioner Murphy's attempt to decentralize the force by making local precinct commanders fully accountable for the actions of the men under their command. It seems to provide a number of advantages for the patrolman, the precinct commander, and the department as a whole. First, in the past no patrolman welcomed the traumatic experience of a statutory hearing at police headquarters. In largely doing away with that, command discipline should greatly improve the morale of the men. Second, outside commands coming into a local precinct to enforce discipline created jurisdictional conflicts between captains and division commanders about their authority to direct and control men under their command. Third, the disciplinary trial machinery of the department has been clogged for years. For example, complaints against individual policemen filed in 1971 were still being heard in 1973, when there was a backlog of 800 cases. Referring only the most serious cases to headquarters was expected to decrease delays in trials.[9] In other words; before command discipline was instituted, the department was handling 2400 to 2600 sets of charges per year; something like ten percent of the men in the department were getting charges in the course of the year that had to be handled "downtown." With command discipline, the estimated figure for 1972 was reduced to 500 to 700 charges per year.

Finally, it should be clear that, with the sole authority to discipline his men, the captain is given added responsibility for the activities and actions of his men. He is held responsible for policemen under his command found sleeping on duty, and for corruption during patrol time. There are, however, checks on his freedom to discipline. He must file quarterly reports with the chief inspector and the first deputy commissioner's office enumerating the types of cases he has handled, classifying them according to type of infraction.

Another type of control is carried out by the Internal Affairs

Division (IAD), which is also part of the Inspectional Services Bureau. The IAD usually focuses on cases of alleged corruption of individual policemen and dereliction of duty. This control limits the opportunity of policemen to supplement their income by petty larceny, graft, bribes, and extortion. And it limits the policeman's opportunities to act out his frustrations against such controls when such activity includes bribery, violence, and abuse. The men who carry out this assignment are police undercover agents or "secret" police, and are referred to as "the gestapo."[10]

All our police recognize the need for some type of police surveillance because corruption does exist in the department. One police officer argues that the IAD is necessary because it protects the cop from his own temptations and fallibility:

Human nature is really a base thing. Basically we are very animal. We just want to grab. We just want to take. We aren't very nice people. That's true. So I say we overrate human nature. So we must fall back on some kind of discipline. Right now we are going through this stage in the department. We have to scare the hell out of the men. You are going to jail unless you obey the rules. . . . So you have to have the IAD. You have to have a gestapo, so to speak. People are going to do things wrong. We have had policemen who have exposed themselves in school yards. They are sick men. This happens We have allegations of cops dealing in narcotics. . . . So we have to have the IAD but it is a distasteful job. The trouble is that when you join the IAD you are not only isolated from society because you are a cop but you are isolated from the department. (35)

But although they recognize that some policemen may be corrupt, police officers are angry at the IAD because *all* policemen are subject to police surveillance.

Like I said there is corruption and the IAD tries to contain it or handle it or do what they can. Even an honest cop—a reasonably honest cop—knows or fears that what he might do may be interpreted as corruption. It's like they have a camera on you. Maybe you hand a guy a summons and they think it's something else. This is the way they think. It's like a big brother kind of thing. It's like 1984! He's watching me and you say somebody is watching him. But people don't like to be watched. And this is especially true if you are honest. And of course, if you are dishonest, you definitely don't want to be watched. (19)

Another respondent believes that honest policemen are betrayed by their superiors and duped into being corrupt by the unscrupulous methods used by the IAD to maintain discipline.

Unfortunately the only person that is affected by the Internal Affairs Division is the honest cop who is out there doing his job. Because he is the only guy who comes into contact with the IAD. Let us say that I am in Internal Affairs, and I am going to try and fool you. I have got narcotics and I am going to try and lock you up. I am going to try and bribe you to see where you will go or not. And if you do—I've got you! And the cop who does nothing never comes into contact with Internal Affairs. So again, who gets hurt? The guy who is doing his job. (25)

Although policemen submit out of fear of punishment to the supervision we have described, an underlying attitude of bitterness, skepticism, and mistrust remains. Policemen express an unwillingness to trust or confide in superior officers, and have learned to suspect the motivations of people dressed in civilian clothes:

You don't know who is who. You'll see a cop come into the precinct in civilian clothes and the guys will start asking who is he, where did he come from, what's his story. It's really ridiculous but this is what the IAD has created. (16)

The joke now is don't talk to anybody. Just stay by yourself. You don't know who you are talking to. You can't confide in anybody. (18)

This is especially true for newcomers. Although newcomers have always been regarded with suspicion and distrust by the other members of the department, the psychological climate created by the IAD seems to have intensified police distrust of these men.

The only time distrust comes into the picture is if you are a new man in the precinct. Sometimes it takes you up to a year or two years before anyone will really start talking to you or come over to you and carry on a conversation. However, not trusting the new man today is the result of the Internal Affairs or the PCIU, which is the Police Commissioners Investigative Unit. These guys are sent out to get a cop in trouble. So there has to be mixed feelings about the new guy. They don't know about him, his background, and they haven't had enough time to find out, to work with him, to see whether he is on the up and up. (25)

Other policemen feel that the IAD has broken down the personal trust and confidence that has always been the basis for a good working relationship among policemen.

You can't trust who you are working with nowadays. A fellow I work with in the Bronx, I just found this out the other day, he's got fifteen years on the job and works for the IAD. Now, this guy must have gotten jammed up. And you figure he got jammed up and he is trying to bargain his way out by sinking another cop. This is how they work. And particularly now, I work in an area where 600 guys came from different parts of the city all in one area [midtown]. So who can you trust? You don't know anyone or anybody. You don't even know their background. You don't know anyone who has worked with them before. So in a normal situation you would say he is a cop, and he is my buddy. I can count on him. But not anymore—there is a lot of distrust. You can't trust anybody. . . . (38)

Personal trust above all means that a policeman can depend on his partner on the job regardless of how he feels about him. *It does not mean trust in the enforcement of the law.* A policeman cannot trust his partner if he is required to denounce him. Thus, there is a kind of built-in mistrust in personal relationships among police officers unless they collude in closing their eyes to corruption.

> Now according to the rules and procedures of the department—and this is reinforced by the IAD—if my partner does something wrong I'm to turn him in. This is the rule. Now I'm with a guy for six years. I am with him longer than I am with my wife. If he does something wrong I have to turn him in. This is what the IAD wants [laughing]. What they are asking is impossible from where they are recruiting from. They have lowered standards. They are not paying you enough. Yet what they want is ethics—the highest that there is. They want all of this but you don't get people, the average person, to turn your partner in. I think they should recruit from the priesthood. . . . (16)

GUIDELINES AND RESTRAINTS ON POLICE BEHAVIOR.   Policemen resent being "advised" by their officers to "let it lie" or to "play it cool" when a city area is under great tensions. They also resent the precise guidelines issued by the top brass that prevent them from misusing their power during confrontations with civil and political dissenters while being provoked with insults and vile language and taunted with threats to their authority and manhood.[11]

> During the riots of 1964 we were looking for leadership. But we were told to cool it—not to make arrests—to turn around and act as if we didn't see it. They told us not to get involved. (5)

> One day a sergeant in charge of a detail of one to ten men up in Harlem after the riots tells us to take the following order: Hands Off! Do Nothing! Say Nothing to These People! So I said, if we do nothing why don't we just sign out? (1)

Policemen are restrained from using their authority against protestors, and often regardless of whether protestors are peaceful or provocative:

> One night I went over to the 2-5 [25th precinct] when the Young Lords had taken a church over. And we were told by the captain not to make arrests under any circumstances in the area involving the Young Lords. (30)

> I recall near the United Nations we had a demonstration. I recall having arrested a group of demonstrators. And we had these demonstrators in the vans and we were told to let them go. And this order came down from the Mayor's office. (5)

But policemen are particularly angry at the "hypocrisy" of their political leaders who allow blacks during race riots to systematically plunder and loot and burn white-owned enterprises under the guise that a few broken windows and a few lootings are far better than giving the blacks some new excuse to flare up. They ask how they can tell a merchant who is trying to make a living that the department has decided to sacrifice his store, and his business, and his life's work because it is far better than to incite the neighborhood. They don't see it, and probably never will.

> Going back to the Harlem riots. When we were on duty there we were told in very specific terms not to take police action. And here there were people walking in and out of stores with merchandise they had taken. And how about the store owners in those areas. Don't they deserve protection? Then we are told to give peddler's citations for not having a permit. Now here is a guy who is not on welfare. He works very hard to scratch out an existence for himself under the most difficult conditions. And he is working honestly to make a dollar. But you are told to go out there and beat his brains in because he doesn't have a permit. But a rioter—I am told not to bother him. Why? (13)

Despite this resentment, superior officers give orders and policemen carry them out. In a paramilitary organization like the police, the only way to get conscientious performance is to secure immediate acceptance of commands. It is the policeman's place not to question orders but to carry them out. If a superior officer is unreasonable with these directives he can push a cop pretty hard. But the cop has to restrain himself or get a complaint and face a disciplinary hearing. A disciplinary hearing is a great teacher.

They say [at demonstrations] your mother is this or your father is that . . . and some cops can't take it. When you come on the job you are going to be called every name in the book, and your family and friends. This is true especially when you are in uniform at demonstrations. But you have to cut it off and pretend you don't hear it. (31)

Nevertheless, there is a small minority of policemen that express an incipient revolt against such orders, and an unwillingness to cooperate with their superior officers.

If I was involved in a situation and somebody came up to me and told me not to make an arrest I would seriously question it. And even if I felt that you might suffer severe repercussions. . . . Nobody will ever assault me. Nobody will ever lay their hands on me, and nobody will ever tell me not to arrest a person who has laid their hands on me. I am not a punching bag. And I am not out there to be made a punching bag. (26)

You take an oath to make arrests when you see violations committed when you are in the academy, but in many riot situations we have heard indirect orders given not to step on toes, turn your back, look the other way, consider the whole picture before you make an arrest; this is malarky in my opinion. I just am not for it, and I mean it when I say this, there is no inspector there, there's no DCI, there's no police commissioner that's ever going to tell me a direct order to my face to lay off or turn away from a crime I see committed. (10)

And in a few cases, this frustration leads to aggression toward supervisors, a revolt against departmental directives, and even insubordination.

> The majority of the guys are war veterans. . . . And they are not used to being pushed around especially when you have a uniform on. So a lot of guys are very uptight about this. And they find it intolerable. They are at a point now where they don't care what the bosses say to them anymore. If they feel endangered or even if the crowd comes close to them they are just going to wade into them. . . . So you will see in the papers from time to time where a cop just blew his top—will react in an extreme way to a very mild provocation because they are very tense and uptight. The guys just don't care anymore. They say arrest me. I got a lawyer [PBA attorney]. (31)

The following incident is a good example of police revolt against duly constituted political authority:

> I remember during the Harlem riots in 1964 I saw guys down there shooting up at the roof tops trying to pin down people throwing bricks. . . . And a lieutenant came along and said, "Put that gun away. You have no authority to fire!" The cop told him, "If you are afraid of getting hurt with gunfire around here, then get the hell out of here. I'm a cop sent up here to do a job and I am going to do a job." At that point the lieutenant would ordinarily prefer charges against him. But this was a common thing in 1964; cops telling bosses don't try and stop me. Cops are refusing to listen to bosses. (28)

In the final analysis, all these responses reflect an organizational struggle between the police bureaucracy that tries to maintain democratic controls and discipline over police behavior, and policemen who are trying to enlarge their bureaucratic freedom at the expense of the political freedom of their clientele.

CIVILIAN COMPLAINT REVIEW BOARDS. In 1966 Mayor Lindsay, as part of a campaign promise, instituted a seven-member civilian complaint review board to investigate and to evaluate civilian allegations of police misconduct: unnecessary or excessive use of force, abuse of authority, discourtesy, insulting language, and language, conduct, or behavior demeaning to a person's racial, ethnic, or religious status. Three of the board's members were appointed by the police commissioner from within the department. Four members were civilians appointed by the mayor from outside the city government on the basis of recommendations made by an eleven-member panel appointed by the mayor to screen and suggest candidates. The board had investigative and advisory powers, not judicial authority. It was an aid to the police commissioner in making his decisions. It in no way diminished his authority and responsibility to maintain discipline and control over the department. In that sense it was not an "independent" review board, free of any ties from the police department. Furthermore, the board functioned in private; its deliberations and recommendations were confidential. The police officer was informed of the complaint and allegations against him, and he was given the right to counsel. Liberal groups considered the board "balanced, just, and humane."[12]

Nevertheless, the board was defeated at the polls in a citywide referendum on November 8, 1966 after four months of operation. Its defeat was spearheaded by the Patrolmen's Benevolent Association, which had mounted an effective, well-financed public relations campaign with television jingles alluding to the spector of black violence. It was argued that such a board would handcuff the police, diminish the police commissioner's discretion, demoralize the rank and file, and interfere with the power of the police to make arrests, and to take what the police considered "proper police action." Civilians were said to be unqualified to judge and evaluate police action, and, insofar as they were "leftists" or "left-leaning racists," likely to be biased against the police (the board included black and Puerto Rican members). It was also charged that civilians on the board represented outside interference with the self-direction and autonomy of the police, and this pernicious influence was condemned as "politics."[13]

Today's civilian complaint review board is completely staffed by police personnel—it is from top to bottom a *police department* review board without any outside civilian participation. But strangely enough the emotional impact of the board remains. Our police still do not care for it; they feel it is essentially the same board that was defeated in the referendum.

> We have people just looking over our shoulders just waiting for us to make mistakes. We have the civilian complaint review board which Mr. Lindsay actually didn't put across when the public supported us. The public was against a civilian review board but actually Lindsay has put a board in there. It's close to what he wanted. And we feel he got just about what he wanted. (17)

It seems from the above that it is not a question of whether a review board includes civilians. It seems that a review board, whatever its shape or form, is seen as interfering with police affairs, including the thorough investigation and impartial evaluation of allegations of police misconduct. It also sullies the ideal image of the policeman as a person whose authority is not challenged. And it makes him subject to restraints, having to follow procedures and to make arrests according to the book. The policeman seems to have a romanticized version of being above the law, but whenever he runs into the law he feels handicapped.[14]

> I saw on the news last night an incident at the 112th precinct. The police had barricades up there because the people there were picketing. And the people were told to picket orderly but they went ahead and broke through the barricades. So the cops had to use physical force and one of the big guys up there said he was going to put in a civilian complaint to the CCRB. And that's the way it is anymore. You can't do anything anymore. You have to be careful of what you say and do. Because nobody is going to back you and if you hang, you hang all by yourself—even to the extent of being arrested. You have to be very careful today. The guys feel they can't do a job. Because if you do your job you will end up in trouble. . . . (24)

One police officer goes so far as to suggest that an internal review board takes away his civil rights or even his due process—a condition many police officers have apparently not been willing to give to others.

Well, as a policeman you are handled like a second-class citizen. You have no rights like a normal person would have. You are at everyone else's discretion. Anything that is said by anyone against you—anyone who makes an allegation against you —they are assumed to be right and you are assumed to be wrong whether you are or not. I have been to the Civilian Complaint Review Board twice [the respondent has been on the job for two years]. Both times because I issued a summons to a person. Once I gave a man a summons who was parked at a bus stop. I was on foot patrol that afternoon. . . . I had to go downtown and answer an allegation that I harassed this man, that I used obscene language. And the person didn't have to appear there [at the review board] which is I think against the Constitution. If a man is going to say something against you he should say it to your face and it should be proven. So this is the reason I feel that the policeman is not treated fairly. Because no matter what he does, he is always guilty without being proven guilty. (25)

But much of the criticism was directed not at the review board itself (which many police officers were reluctantly willing to admit was quite benign and "just") but at the administration that encouraged the public to bring forward legitimate grievances regarding police misconduct.

The administration has made it very easy for the civilian populace to make complaints and allegations. (Can you tell me something about this?) I have been on this job for six and a half years, and I have received seven or eight of these complaints. I received a couple for brutality, abusive language, and abuse of police powers. The last three complaints that I received were all civilian complaints for abuse of police powers. These three complaints all involved traffic summonses. The people felt that they shouldn't have received the summonses, and because they felt this I was supposedly abusive because I issued the summonses. (15)

Others direct their criticism at the public, which has become less reluctant to criticize police behavior.[15] Perhaps this reflects a growing confidence in a democratic community that the department will deal with complaints justly.

Everybody is so conscious of their rights. "You have no right to search me," they say. "I'll make a complaint out against you." I remember a friend of mine who was given a complaint because the guy who made the complaint said my friend gave him a dirty look. This was dismissed, of course, by the civilian review board, but it shows how easy it is today to give the policeman a complaint. (5)

In addition, the demands of many blacks from the central cities and their increased militancy in resisting traditional police brutality, together with the increasing political powers of blacks, have caused this minority group to make more complaints against abuse of police authority, discourtesy, and racial slurs. Thus policemen are far more careful today when they take official action against blacks. The following report is typical:

I think that the cop today is afraid. He is afraid of doing his job. And it goes back to changes in the law and the civil rights thing. You've got to be careful with minority groups. If a guy is Negro you are afraid to get involved. Because if you get involved you may end up getting a complaint which is unwarranted, or brought up for charges for manhandling some fine citizen. (2)

To be sure, the vast majority of civilian complaints filed against New York City policemen over the years have been found to be unsubstantiated.[16] Nevertheless, a few police officers believe that even after a complaint is cleared by the board (that is, unsubstantiated or "conciliated," meaning that the complainant presumably was satisfied but the complaint was not found to be substantiated), a notation of the complaint is made in the officer's career folder. This notation is thought to present problems when it comes to promotion or reassignment. As a result, policemen show reluctance to take police action when they feel it may lead to complaints not found to be substantiated. For example:

When I worked in a radio car around Amsterdam Avenue, we got a complaint around two o'clock in the morning that there was a dispute between a tenant and a landlord. So we go there and I take down all the information and I put a padlock on the door. I tell the parties to go to court. A tenant tells me that the woman was no longer living with her husband and did not pay the rent, et cetera. A week goes by and I get called into the office. They had received a complaint from this woman that I had raped her and her kid! I said, "Oh, my God!" They were ready to suspend me and bring me up for charges. They finally investigated this and found out the charge was unwarranted. They found out she was a prostitute, and that she was living a common-law life, and her boyfriend had a record, and he was wanted in Baltimore. So they arrested all of them. But now, even to this day, I got a letter in my record. Even though it is stamped unwarranted, it raises questions in the minds of those who read it. When I got this detail they pulled out my record and asked about it. So, many guys are afraid to get involved because of these letters of complaint. (2)

Such accusations indicate how policemen reproduce their fears under certain circumstances. Actually, Sanford D. Garelik's *Bill of Rights* for policemen (Garelik was a former Chief Inspector of the department) protects the men from precisely this type of punitive atmosphere and safeguards all their legal rights. If the allegations are found to be unsubstantiated, the policeman receives a letter that no notation of the complaint will be made in his record file.

RESTRICTIONS ON THE POLICE USE OF FIREARMS. The police gun is a weapon of violence that everyone understands may sometimes be

used. Like the hangman and soldier, the policeman may legally
inflict death on members of a society.

The gun is a problem.[17] Policemen have traditionally been permitted to use their weapon whenever they had "reasonable cause"
to believe that a fleeing felon was dangerous or whenever they "suspected" that a crime had been committed. Because of this discretionary use of the weapon, controlling "improper and unnecessary
violence" has been a serious problem of enlightened police administrators and their democratic officials as far back as 1931 when
the Wickersham Committee criticized the "police violence" then
routinely used by many police departments.

In 1966 the issue was raised again. A national crime commission,
formally known as the President's Commission on Law Enforcement
and Administration of Justice, observed that one out of ten policemen (in a sample of 450 police officers covering a total of 850 eight-
hour tours of duty) had used "unnecessary force" and police violence
against whites and blacks in slum areas of Washington, Boston, and
Chicago.[18] The Commission made the following recommendations.
(1) Deadly force should not be used against any suspect unless the
arresting officer's safety or the safety of someone else was endangered. (2) Such force should never be used "on mere suspicion"
that a crime had been committed. (3) Policemen should not "fire
on felony suspects when less force could be used." (4) Warning
shots should never be used. (5) Detailed written reports were to
be required on all discharge of firearms. (6) The Justice Department should withhold from law enforcement agencies federal funds
for new weapons if these agencies failed to incorporate "appropriate
restraints and controls" on the police use of firearms.[19]

All of these recommendations were incorporated in New York
State's revised Penal Law in 1967. The Penal Law states in effect
that police officers may use their weapons only when their life is in
danger or to defend the life of another person from deadly force.
One respondent puts it in the following terms:

If I see some guy break a store window across the street and I
can't get to him in time . . . I can't shoot him. I can't shoot

him because of changes in the penal law regarding firearms.
You can't even shoot a warning shot. You can't use deadly force
against a suspect unless your life or someone else's safety is
endangered. (2)

Needless to say, policemen are generally hostile to the new penal
code because it prevents them from doing what they want. Moreover,
they believe that it creates the conditions for lawlessness—an argument that appeals to the fears and prejudices of many sectors of the
population. An example:

I personally feel that the old law of being able to shoot at a
fleeing felon is better for the simple reason that certain types of
crime like muggings and purse snatchings have increased since
they passed the new law. When they know that they can't get
hurt there is nothing stopping them. They stick their tongue
out at you after they have mugged somebody even after you
tell them to stop or you will shoot because they know you
won't. Under the old law ninety percent of them would stop
when you said, "Halt or I'll shoot!" (1)

One police officer cynically remarks that he worries little about
the use of his weapon within the framework of the penal code because the code has appropriated all of his authority.

The Penal Law in 1967 took a lot of responsibility away from
me. I worry very little now about the use of my firearm. (I
don't understand this statement.) I can't use my gun! And if
you can't use your gun you don't have to worry about it! We
have been told: you will not use your gun. You will not use
your gun unless you are defending yourself. And then you have
to be *sure* you are defending yourself. (15)

He goes on to indicate concern over the implications of this revised law:

There are some guys who are walking around with a gun that
doesn't even work. It's one piece of rust. And this is simply

because they know they can't use it. I'm not telling you something that hasn't happened. This has all taken place in the few
years that I've been on the job. (15)

If he fires his weapon he is immediately transferred out of the
area or reassigned until an investigation has been conducted to determine whether the firing was justifiable under the revised penal rule.
Such a policy is considered unjustified and intolerable.

There was an order out that I didn't think was justified. If you
did use your gun when you shot somebody you would be transferred from the area and assigned to the Detective Division
while they investigate the shooting. Consequently an officer did
shoot someone and was assigned to Borough Headquarters for
a week doing clerical duty. I personally did not take this job
to sit in a clerical office shuffling paper work because I shot
somebody in the performance of my duty. I can't accept this
concept. If a man is shot, most likely, he's shot for a reason
or good cause. To me that's good enough. (15)

A few policemen believe that the new penal code is sufficiently
ambiguous in its wording to lead to confusion as to when an officer
is justified in using his weapon. This leads to hesitation, and hesitation can only place the officer's life in danger.

You see the penal law has got some men snowed. By snowed I
mean baffled, because of the wording of it. And the justification
for drawing the gun is confused in their minds. And as a result,
many of them hesitate. And the old saying is, he who hesitates
is lost. (19)

Others disagree. As a practical matter, policemen can tell when
their lives are in danger and they will not hesitate to shoot out of
self-preservation.

I honestly think that's just a phony argument [concerning the
confusion over the Penal Code]. Because when it comes right

down to it you know when you are in danger or not. Let's be honest. We're human beings. None of us want to go into the box any sooner than necessary. So when we feel we are in danger the average cop feels he would rather shoot and be around to explain to the Grand Jury why he shot than hesitate and have some cop explain to his wife why he will never come home again. I think this is just a "cop out" they use. They just don't like the changes in the law. (28)

I would rather get a complaint than get six feet in the ground. If you want to throw me off the job, fine, but at least I'm still alive. So in a way it's simply survival. (14)

I would have no hesitancy in firing if I believed my life was in danger. And I will go before any tribunal and explain my actions. Because the last thing I want to do is to have an inspector's funeral. (26)

It seems reasonable to conclude that policemen are demoralized because they have lost their politically protective position. No longer do they have the independence of self-government or autonomy that once allowed them to operate by their most direct and efficient means without outside interference. Restrictions on the use of firearms, civilian review boards, surveillance, and all the other regulations, forms, and controls we have described are threats to the special protective position of a relatively strong bureaucratic group. This accounts for much of the victimization and demoralization typically expressed by the police. To criticize these bureaucratic controls is tantamount to asserting that the department has let the policemen down. It is not surprising that all the attempts by the Police Department to increase morale have failed.

Moreover, the respondents feel that the agency which has increased power and control over the police is a political administration that is more responsive to the black and Puerto Rican population than it is to police aspirations. This is why policemen are antagonistic toward the department and the city administration.

At the same time, the increase in the black population, which was accompanied by all the crime associated with a new immigrant group, together with a militancy that resists traditional controls over crime, caused the police to feel caught between two millstones. The mayor and the upper reaches of the police administration restricted in principle the rights of the policemen to deal with violence at the same time that violence was increasing. Thus the police feel they are handcuffed. They are subject to political interference. They cannot do their job. And yet they bear the burden for the failure of being unable to do that job.

In general this is not the way police work presented itself to whites at the time of entry, who believed, that they could define and undertake the job to suit their inclinations, and that the job would help them achieve their identity. But the job does not reassure the policeman—white or black—of his self-perceptions and expectations. To this extent, both the department and society have betrayed the white policeman's attempts to achieve the social benefits, prestige, and identity toward which he was striving.

NOTES

1. See the useful article by Albert J. Reiss, Jr. and David J. Bordua, "Environment and Organization: A Perspective on the Police," in David J. Bordua, ed., *The Police: Six Sociological Essays* (New York: John Wiley & Sons, 1967), pp. 25–55.

2. I draw on the Police Department Table of Organization as reported by Robert D. McFadden, "Patrol Chief Typifies Murphy's New Top Aids," *The New York Times*, August 31, 1971.

3. Ibid.

4. The special powers of the police in terms so described are briefly discussed by Sydney C. Cooper, former Chief of Inspectional Services of the New York City Police Department, in an interview with David Burnham, "A Corruption Fighter Retires Undeterred After 31 Years on Force," *The New York Times*, July 22, 1972.

5. See, for example, Isidore Silver, "Restraining The Police," *The Massachusetts Review*, Vol. 40, No. 3 (Summer 1970), pp. 587–600.

6. For a systematic discussion of "ringing in" as well as other types of controls described in terms of problematic situations facing the police see John H. McNamara, "Uncertainties in Police Work: The Relevance of Police Recruits' Backgrounds and Training," in David J. Bordua, op. cit., pp. 163–252.

7.   See, for example, Robert E. Tomasson, "Police Deride and Fear Investigators," *The New York Times*, September 1, 1971.

8.   Here I draw on an interview with a high-ranking police officer who works in the Planning Division of the New York City Police Department. See also Lacey Fosburgh's report on the concept of command discipline in "Police Commanders Get New Power To Discipline Men," *The New York Times*, October 4, 1971.

9.   See Lacey Fosburgh, op. cit.

10.   See David Burnham, "Police Use Agents To Test Own Men," as reported in *The New York Times*, July 29, 1971.

11.   For an interesting report on police reactions to the strategy of restraint during the 1972 Republican Convention in Miami Beach see Jon Nordheimer, "Some Policemen Bitter Over a Strategy of Restraint," *The New York Times*, August 24, 1972.

12.   I draw on an excellent account of the New York Civilian Complaint Review Board by its former chairman, Algernon D. Black, *The People and the Police* (New York: McGraw-Hill, 1968).

13.   Ibid.

14.   A nice fictionalized version of this romantic notion is given by T. Mike Walker (a writer-cop), *Voices from the Bottom of the World* (New York: Grove Press, 1969).

15.   For an interesting report on the record number of complaints made against policemen during 1972 see "3,700 Complaints On Police Filed," *The New York Times*, January 1, 1973.

16.   See Bernard Cohen, *The Police Internal Administration of Justice in New York City*, R-621-NYC, The New York City–Rand Institute, November 1970, pp. 24–28.

17.   The tools of the trade of police officers are carefully described by Jonathan Rubinstein in his excellent ethnography of the police, *City Police* (New York: Ballantine Books, 1973), pp. 275–290.

18.   See David Burnham, "Police Violence: A Changing Pattern," as reported in *The New York Times*, July 7, 1968.

19.   Algernon D. Black, op. cit., pp. 144–147.

4

Disclosures of Police Corruption
Undermine the Police Image

The image of the policeman as a knight in shining armor expertly protecting society from the criminal offender is contradicted by the evidence of organized police corruption. Investigations of police corruption are so threatening to the image that police officers often consider investigations more injurious than the practice of corruption. The police counter this threat to their legitimacy by emphasizing the danger in their work—the possibility of injury and death. Their lives are on the line. This law-and-order ideology, insofar as it has community support, permits the police to indulge in nonviolent crimes themselves. It almost gives the police the special right to supplement their income by payoffs, cooping, and a variety of illegal activities, provided that they do not "goof off" when faced with violence.

This may tie in with the policemen's racial beliefs that the violent criminal is likely to be black and the nonviolent criminal is likely to be white. Since the police emphasize the violence, danger, and heroism of their work, they may consider violence and payoffs directed against blacks with payoffs from whites to be justified.

Payoffs, bribery, extortion, and other forms of bureaucratic illegality may involve not only patrolmen and other precinct personnel, but also detectives and division heads. Those in charge of law enforcement themselves violate the law. Almost every police officer who has risen to a top supervisory or command position has had many opportunities for systematic or patterned evasions of the rules. In the cycle of his career the police officer often moves from rule violator to rule enforcer. But because he often comes to the latter role with "unclean hands," it becomes increasingly difficult to enforce the rules, since violations are institutionalized. An entire group or precinct, itself engaged in illegalities and misfeasance, knows the police officer to be an offender. He will then find it very difficult to enforce the rules on those with whom he has colluded in institutionalized crime.

But more than law violation is at stake. When John Newton Mitchell, the former Attorney General of the United States, is recognized as a law violator, it is no longer John Mitchell but the law itself that is in the hands of criminals. When Richard Nixon gets involved, then the whole issue of law and order is compromised. And like George Orwell's 1984, the language used to legitimate a society's values loses its power of distinction, and ("law and order" becomes a crime).

In the same way, police officers involved in systematic crimes must find some higher dimension to justify the crime. For Richard Nixon it was "national security." For white police officers it is protecting society from violence—and that violence is perpetrated by blacks. Thus the threat of violence allows the police officer to do almost anything in the cause of containing violence, whether it is directly related to law enforcement or to gaining special advantages from the performance of some of his duties.

But how does one reform a police system when a substantial and undetermined part is replete with corruption and illegality? If one systematically disciplined and punished all corrupt police officers and those who tolerated corruption, there would be too few to carry out the police function. Yet such revelations as the Knapp Commission findings[1] make it imperative that commanders and political leaders fire and punish at least conspicuous violators of police codes.

Assuming that the political officials are sincere, the most that they can do is selectively transfer, punish, and reorganize division after division, precinct after precinct with the hope that these actions will outweigh the continuous law violations and "coverups" that follow immediately after the heat of exposure is dampened.

Yet these patterns of exposure, punishment, and transfer cannot be accomplished in any one short period of time for several reasons. First, those who would control law violations by the police are themselves subject to the constraints of legality. Gaining evidence to justify prosecution of policemen is as difficult as any other kind of case because the police know what it is to conceal evidence. Also, it is difficult in such prosecutions to find untainted investigators.

Secondly, law enforcement must continue even while the police department is being investigated, depleted, and reorganized. Too many prosecutions at once would disrupt those normal operations. The amount of reform therefore must be limited so that normal operations can proceed. But if some semblance of law and order is to prevail within the department, the process of investigation, prosecution, and reorganization must be continuous. If this process were to stop one could expect a further rise in police illegality. Thus even within the department, eternal vigilance is the price of personal, individual liberty to define and undertake the job in one's own way.

THE KNAPP COMMISSION AND POLICE CORRUPTION. It has become a truism to say that corruption exists in the Police Department. Every time an agency has looked for police corruption it has found it. As far back as 1894, the Lexow Committee, an investigative and quasi-prosecutory body, found corruption among the police. This was also true of the Mazet hearings in 1900, which revealed that widespread inefficiency and corruption plagued urban police forces in the United States.[2]

But unlike other bodies of its kind, the Knapp Commission found that police corruption was a "disease" of epidemic proportions that involved more than sixty percent of the police officers in the department.[3] It was not a question of a few rotten apples, as police public relations would like us to believe. The barrel itself was rotten.[4] The Knapp Commission differed from its predecessors in several other ways. It supplied information to local and federal prosecutors so that legal action could be taken against those implicated in the hearings.[5] It was not created from outside, but by John V. Lindsay, the first mayor to take the full responsibility for corrution.[6] And partly as a result of the commission's findings, and partly as a result of his own determination to root out corruption, Commissioner Patrick J. Murphy, during his relatively short tenure in office, did more to clean up corruption in the department than all the previous city police administrators put together.

Following charges in the *New York Times* that widespread police corruption existed throughout the city, the Knapp Commission was established in May 1970 by Mayor Lindsay to conduct an independent and thorough inquiry to ascertain the truth. Headed by Whitman Knapp, its chairman, a Wall Street lawyer, and Michael F. Armstrong, and sustained by City Council and federal funds and grants of approximately $700,000, the five-man panel was given the authority to subpoena witnesses.[7]

Ironically, the Knapp Commission's first interim report criticized the Lindsay Administration for its failure to investigate allegations of serious misconduct when informed by federal investigators between 1968 and 1970 that seventy-two police officers were improperly engaged in the narcotics traffic.[8] The administration was also criticized for failing to act when informed by Sergeant David Durk and Detective Frank Serpico of systematic bribes and other misdeeds among plainclothes gambling-enforcement policemen in the Bronx.[9]

At the same time, Whitman Knapp applauded Police Commissioner Murphy, "one of the great commisioners of this department," for taking more actions to reduce police corruption than any other commissioner.[10]

It is noteworthy that much of the Knapp Commission's interim report was supportive of Murphy's policies—policies that incurred the wrath of the Patrolmen's Benevolent Association, which regarded

Murphy's attempts as smears on the police image and vicious assaults on police morale.

Murphy lectured his commanding officers and the public about how police corruption had undermined police officers' efficiency in fighting crime. He had also issued a confidential memorandum to Police Department brass serving notice that he wanted "every member of the . . . department to be aware that there was no room for compromise with his position of trust." He hoped that the department would have a "bloodless revolution against misconduct and low standards," since the job (anticipating that the Knapp Commission hearings were soon to begin) was going to be done anyway.[11]

In response to the failure of his commanders to heed his warnings, Murphy introduced a number of radical procedural reforms referred to by the press as "Murphy's maxims." He changed the methods and organization of the patrolmen assigned to enforce gambling, prostitution, and liquor laws. This allowed Murphy to achieve greater control and supervision over investigative personnel, while minimizing conditions conducive to corrupting influences. He told his commanding officers that they would be held accountable for the wrongdoings of their men (the command discipline concept), and warned them that they would also be held responsible for any increase in crime within their own precincts and districts. He tightened supervision throughout the chain of command. He more than tripled the number of internal police working in the Internal Affairs Division. He transferred and demoted hundreds of policemen to disrupt established routines and corrupt habits of mind, and promoted others for their work against police corruption. Murphy hoped to create a psychological climate in which every police officer would realize that it was "his moral as well as legal obligation to take action when he knows or suspects that the other officer has compromised his principles."[12] In short, efforts to elevate the professionalism of the department and to root out corruption began to affect deeply the attitudes of policemen and the daily work of the Police Department.

In July 1971, at the end of the commission's eleven-month investigation, Mr. Knapp reported that a "substantial number" of police officers were thieves, cunning predators, and good shakedown artists engaged in a variety of criminal acts including stealing, extortion, graft, payoffs, and drug selling.

Police member associations reacted swiftly to these allegations. Edward Kiernan, then president of the PBA, stated unequivocally that the charges were preposterous and unjust, and that the only answer was a direct refutation of these charges. This was the beginning of a series of retaliations, attacks, and counterattacks that ran the course of the Knapp investigation.

In September 1971, Kiernan put the PBA on record against the drive to banish corruption from the police force.[14] In addition, the PBA sued unsuccessfully to have the commission found illegal under the terms of the city charter, and dozens of PBA delegates and members tried in vain to curb the panel's subpoena power on the ground that the constitutional rights of those answering the subpoenas would be violated.

Deputy Chief Inspector Eli Lazarus, the president of the Captains' Endowment Association, also denounced the commission's allegations and told its members not to fill out a commission "corruption assessment" report that required commanders to state in detail their finances: to list all bank accounts, safe deposit boxes, insurance policies, and the number of automobiles, boats, and airplanes they might own. Lazarus was reported to have said that the assessment report violated the fundamental rights enshrined in constitutional guarantees: the right to privacy against agencies that "resort to belated devices of questionable propriety."[15] His denunciation followed in the wake of a protest by patrolmen on the Upper East Side in having to complete a detailed financial questionnaire of their own.

On October 13, 1971, the Sergeants' Benevolent Association filed suit in State Supreme Court to bar the Knapp hearings that were scheduled to begin. Harold H. Melnick, the president of the 2300-member association, charged that the real purpose of the hearings was "to provide antecedent publicity in a circus-like atmosphere for the personal gratification and aggrandizement of those who would seek

to heap further calumny and ridicule on members of the force."[16]
But all of this was a preliminary skirmish to the nine days of
televised hearings and public disclosures by three corrupt "turn
around" policemen detailing blatant, organized, systematic corruption and dozens of acts of misconduct in every police division.
The hearings disclosed that although most policemen were engaged in some form of unlawful behavior, some were more corrupt
("meat eaters") than others ("grass eaters").[17] "Meat eaters,"
while few in number, were well-established operators who aggressively sought large payments of thousands of dollars from narcotics
and gambling. Corruption was their profession; police work was
an incidental activity that more often than not interfered with their
"professional pursuits," causing them distress. The "meat eater's"
place in the criminal underworld was secure and he rated high
among organized crime members. He also had no peers in the department and this was a deep source of "professional pride." He
had arrived in terms of status and economic gain. "Grass eaters"
were petty criminals who accepted gratuities and solicited $5, $10,
and $20 payments from businessmen, contractors, gamblers, and
the like. Although his income was not as high as that of the "meat
eater," within the narrow margins of his relative deprivation he
developed thievery to a fine art.

The hearings also disclosed how police recruits were socialized
into the network of corruption—how and where to get graft, what
restaurants gave free meals, what bars paid off, how to select victims, how to steal without attracting attention. Corruption was so
institutionalized that officers who refused to share in illegal payments
were in danger of becoming outcasts or deviants in their own units,
and were likely to find it difficult and unpleasant to work with
others. Corrupt cops would sometimes try to lead recalcitrant of
ficers who refused to bend to the pressures of wrongdoing into corruption through mutual friends on the force.[18]

The hearings brought out that organized crime, through its control of narcotics, gambling, porno shops, and "gay" bars, was the
single major source of police corruption. Next came legitimate
businesses seeking to ease their way "through the maze of city

ordinances and regulations." Finally came persons caught breaking laws, and small-time criminals like purse snatchers who would attempt to buy their freedom from an arresting officer.[19]

The hearings also ushered in a new phase of hostility between a resistant police bureaucracy and a reform-minded administration.

Mayor Lindsay, who had never endeared himself to the police, was attacked by the PBA for defending the Knapp hearings, for "finding satisfaction in the pressures generated by intensive public scrutiny," and for using the Knapp Commission as "the basis for a major presidential campaign by attracting nationwide attention" as the "corruption-busting Mayor of New York City."[20] Lindsay's lavish praise of the reforms of Murphy also increased police bitterness and hatred toward him.[21]

Commissioner Murphy's antigraft investigations and internal overhauls and shake-ups were viewed by the head of the PBA as "systematic destruction of the finest police department in the world." Moreover, the PBA charged that his performance as police commissioner was "not merely inadequate" but "frightening," and urged him to resign. Harold H. Melnick, chairman of the Police Department Superior Officers' Council, joined in the attack by charging that Murphy was weakening departmental morale by "administrative innuendo" and "blanket indictment" of the integrity and efficiency of his commanders.[22] Yet the hearings supported Murphy's crackdown on the brass by presenting at least "considerable circumstantial evidence" that they "participated in the same kind of corruption as the men they supervised."[23]

The hearings brought forth charges by the police of the commission's use of "gestapolike" methods to get evidence, namely, the use of photographic and tape-recorded evidence collected by "rogue cops" or "turnabouts" who had been caught in their illegal acts and pressured into becoming "bugged" undercover agents for the commission. These men would go about the city talking to fellow officers in order to implicate them in corruption. They were later denounced as finks or stooges for the commission.[24]

The hearings also had the effect of bringing the Civil Liberties Union to the defense of the police by assailing the hearings as a "civil liberties disaster." The CLU criticized the unlawful methods used to gather evidence, the unreliable testimony offered by police informers "to save their own necks," and the failure of the panel to allow the police to cross examine their accusers, a right given any other person so accused under our Constitution.[25]

Finally, from the police standpoint, the hearings undermined the already low respect and confidence that the public had for them, degraded their function, created divisions within their ranks, and subjected their families and children to ridicule and humiliation.

We now consider how policemen in our study reacted to and were affected by the Knapp hearings. It should be mentioned here that fifteen respondents had been interviewed prior to the televised hearings of October 18, 1971, leaving only twenty-seven men to be questioned on their reactions to the disclosures of systematic corruption and the organization of payoffs.

POLICE VULNERABILITY TO THE OPPORTUNITIES TO BE CORRUPT. The Knapp Commission hearings had a dramatic effect on the way all twenty-seven respondents reacted to the charges of corruption. However, only three of them expressed "shock," "surprise," or even discomfort at the extent of police corruption and wrongdoing.

I said, this is some education [in response to the hearings]. If I wanted to get out on the street and start to steal . . . things that I could never have conceived of in my own head and this guy Phillips [Patrolman Phillips was the principal undercover agent to testify for the commission after being caught arranging a series of bribes for the madam of an East Side brothel] was telling me and everybody in the world. (Are you saying that you never knew this type of thing was going on?) Absolutely not! . . . I just can't believe what he was saying. The way he was going around wheeling and dealing from office to office and setting this contract up and that contract up. It's just so unbelievable to me. (So you were surprised, so to speak?) Yeah. I still can't believe that it was true. It's unbelievable. (34)

A police officer usually knows men from his own platoon, squad, or work schedule (duty chart). When these men are transferred to other platoons or squads he no longer knows what they are up to.

I watched . . . most of [the Knapp proceedings] and I have to say that I was very surprised. Very surprised at Phillips and very surprised at Droge [the second corrupt cop to testify about his personal involvement in bribes and other forms of corruption], who worked in my precinct. I knew of him [Droge] and I saw him and I did speak to him but I never worked with him because he never worked with the same chart as I did. And I really never thought one way or the other about him. I didn't know what was going on or what he was doing. In my precinct we have 150 or 175 guys. Now out of that 150 you have so many men on the day squad and you work, let us say, only every third week, and then you have the few men in the squads that work with you. These are the men you actually work with and you are with all the time. The other men you just see coming or going. So you may know a lot of men in the precinct but I don't know very much about them. (19)

These responses are not surprising. Although corruption is systemic in large organizations, not everyone has the same opportunities to be corrupt. A police officer becomes corrupt when he exploits the opportunities available to him. What, then, are the social factors underlying the opportunities to be corrupt?[26]

First, we must consider the position or branch of the department that the police officer occupies. Plainclothesmen assigned to enforce gambling laws, narcotics officers (narcos) assigned to the Narcotics Division, and detectives assigned to investigative duties all have more opportunities than uniformed patrolmen have. Their work requires direct personal association with gambling and narcotics criminals. Moreover, because they are inconspicuous (they wear street clothes) they can operate illicitly and on a regular basis in areas where they are not known. The twenty-four respondents who were "not surprised" recognize that plainclothes assignments may give opportunities for corruption. As a result, if they want to avoid becoming corrupt they do not accept a plainclothes assignment. Conversely, if they want to maximize their acquisitiveness they may volunteer for that branch of service.

> You could make money off of bookmakers and you could make money on narcotics. And some of the guys would say, "Gee, I wish I was in plainclothes. I could make the money and nobody would bother me." This is the kind of attitude you have on the job. Again, as they said during the Knapp Commission this was true to an extent. This kind of thing was a tradition in the branch of plainclothes. You went into plainclothes and you made money. But a lot of guys didn't go into plainclothes for precisely these same reasons. . . . To make contacts [in plainclothes] you have to go into gin mills and have a few drinks, you have to go into certain places and you have to lay out money. And he's not getting that money back. And I mean this is nothing new. So what happens? You started to rob Peter to pay Paul. (38)

The second factor that influences the opportunities for corruption is the precinct or area in the city to which an officer is assigned. Harlem is known as a haven for dope and numbers money, for example. One respondent replied this way to the question, Were you surprised at the extent of crime that police officers were involved in?

> Not really. When you work in Harlem you see a lot of things. You hear a lot of talk. Every time you make a collar [arrest] guys are offering you hundreds of thousands of dollars. They offer you $5000 to cut them loose. . . . The pressure is heavy in Harlem. (31)

A third factor is the officer's assignment. As one officer described it, a traffic cop has few opportunities to be corrupt, but a motorcycle cop in the same traffic division has far greater opportunities. In fact, his opportunities rival that of the plainclothes branch of the department.

Being in Traffic you have less opportunities to make money
unless, like part of Traffic is motorcycle. The motorcycle guys
must rival plainclothes as far as extra income is concerned
easily. (Why?) While plainclothes has to go around certain
individuals who are known gamblers and are known prostitutes
and who might be watched by the IAD [internal security] without them knowing it, the motorcycle man can chase any car he
wants and make any killing he wants. He can size up a car—
you will never see them stop a Volkswagen—a very, very few
of them anyhow. So he'll chase the Cadillacs, the Oldsmobiles,
the Pontiacs, the Buicks, the big Mercurys, but he won't be that
hot on Mercurys either. There was an old saying in the department: if a guy is smoking a pipe and he's driving a Mercury,
give him a summons because you can't get any money off of
him. There is a stigma attached to a guy who is really a tight-
wad. But anybody like a salesman in a Cadillac or doctors in
Cadillacs or lawyers are pretty good that way. Most of them are
businessmen and they are coming from shows at night and they
are out with their secretaries or things like that—they are always
good for ten [dollars]. I knew cops that wouldn't take less than
twenty for speeds [speeding violations]. . . . I know a guy who
was stupid enough to take a check. The guy had no money. (A
check?) How's that for moxey? . . . (29)

In short, our respondents say that the opportunities that exist on
the street predispose them to be corrupt, and that corruption is difficult or impossible to resist. The implication is that a solution to
this persistent problem is almost beyond their control.[27]

PROTECTIVE PRACTICES IN DEALING WITH CORRUPTION. Although
most of our respondents suspect or admit that there is corruption on
the force and are fully aware of the factors that contribute to corrupting influences, they also develop a repertoire of socially protective strategies or defenses to cope with it.[28] Like everyone else
who wants to avoid appearing in a bad light (that is, having a
misnamed identity), the police use their verbal wit to dispel the
notion that they might be what they have been accused of.[29]

For the individual patrolman, protective strategies are important not only for coping with embarrassing situations on the street that bring into play doubts about their honesty and legitimacy, but also for legitimating an impression they give of themselves as coping with dishonesty on the force.[30] Police corruption is seen as no cause for alarm.

Moreover, when these socially protective strategies are supported and reinforced by persistent in-group norms from which the public is excluded, they create a justificatory context for police misfeasance. They become both *cause* and *consequence* of the police officers' failure to prevent what they know or suspect to be going on about them. In other words, these strategies become socially approved "phobic screens"[31] for mitigating or relieving individual responsibility for the extent of police corruption.

The first strategy is to refuse to recognize that corruption is a serious problem symptomatic of an underlying disease that requires public disclosure.[32] This strategy is given support by the police officers' appeal to secrecy. Continual disclosures of police indiscretions will backfire, creating rather than preventing internal disorder or demoralization.

The Knapp Commission was crying out corruption, corruption, corruption. They publicized it. Even if there was what they say there is, they shouldn't publicize it . . . because it is demoralizing to honest cops to see other cops taking graft, being arrested, et cetera. It doesn't look good. (18)

Well, of course I am against the way it was handled. It shouldn't have been televised. It shouldn't have been set out for the general public to see. Again, I don't think we should wash our dirty linen out in public . . . . I suppose they believe that if the public knows what is going on you are going to have a clean department. It isn't like the FBI where they sweep everything under the rug. We are wide open. (38)

Public disclosures destroy established police relations, which are an index of solidarity, and also destroy chances for gathering information.

The trouble is that police feel they are not going to get any co-operation from the public because of this publicity. People who used to come forth with information will lose confidence in their police. (17)

Our respondents also feel that the Knapp Commission has pro-jected the image of the "corrupt cop" so thoroughly that the entire force is stigmatized.

The trouble is that the general public is accepting this blanket indictment. Because they catch ten or fifteen guys they think that everybody is doing it. And this is not right. The first words out of an instructor's mouth in the Police Academy is, "Don't generalize or stereotype a situation or anybody involved in a situation. If you have a dispute handle that· dispute as an indi-vidual thing—look at both sides of it and handle it as it goes. People are people, and all people are not the same." Now they turn around and say, "Do as I say, not as I do." They are stereo-typing us—they are generalizing on us. I haven't heard the word "alleged" used once on that Knapp Commission report. (20)

Even though the commission stated in its final report that it took great pains to avoid stereotyping all police officers, most of our respondents believe that the report condemned the entire force. Since policemen are required to appear honest in every possible way they can most easily counterattack the commission's findings by mis-interpreting them.[33]

I think the Knapp Commission smeared everybody with a brush and said that everybody is dishonest. I don't know what the department or we as police officers can do to go in there and try to rectify these accusations that were made that every cop is a thief, that all cops go in there and take money or take free meals. (26)

Another protective strategy is to refuse to accept certain types of wrongdoing as corrupt. The policeman justifies "corruption" with a reasoned argument generally involving many inferences that are not shared by those who accuse him of corruption. For example, the Knapp Commission found that the most widespread form of corruption was the acceptance by police officers of gratuities in the form of free meals, drinks ("a cup of coffee"), cigarettes, liquor, beer, and cash payments under the table in return for police favors. Most respondents believe that this is not corruption. Eating "on the arm" [for free] is a perquisite of the job and is considered to be within the realm of police propriety ["safe and clean"]. Anything beyond that—taking narcotics money, shaking down prostitutes, and so forth—is considered deviant or "unsafe and not clean."[34]

> Take this guy Droge when he said that every cop in the 80th precinct was crooked and there were only two honest cops. I think it depends on what you mean by honesty. I think it's ridiculous to call a guy a thief for taking a cup of coffee or a sandwich. . . . It's different, however, if you shake down a motorist. I'm against that. (26)

> You might jump out of the car and get a cup of coffee on the arm. I don't know why you should have to pay. Offer the money, by all means. But if he wants to give it to you there's nothin' wrong with a cup of coffee. (21)

> They are finding out little things that go on, like a cup of coffee, and I don't think they are so bad. I think guys who take money for narcotics or from prostitutes should be gotten out of the job. (18)

To overcome or rationalize any objection to eating for nothing, the police officer argues that it is simply a formality, a part of police-proprietor relations. The free meal has the importance of ritual and ceremony; it is part of an etiquette that makes for increased mutual respect, and gives the police officer the satisfaction that he is wel-

comed. It also serves as a form of accommodation. Small store-
keepers contribute to their survival in the inner city by giving police
officers credit in the form of free meals and/or cash. In return,
they receive extra or better service than they would normally get.
Small business persons also expect police officers to overlook minor
traffic violations. Patrons may also be allowed to park and double-
park illegally in front of their establishments.

Like this thing brought out in the Knapp Commission as far as
meals. Like eating for nothing, or getting a cup of coffee for
nothing. Maybe it's not right, but the old proverb says: One
hand washes the other. . . . I mean if this man wants to give you
things from his store this is nobody's business but his. Now, he
has given it to me, let us say, so I give his store a little extra
attention. So I walk down the block and try his door to see if
it's open. There is nothing criminally wrong with that. (25)

The guy who gives the coffee and the sandwich is overjoyed to
have you come in. The owner of the store couldn't get that type
of protection anywhere. (26)

This behavior is also justified by suggesting that it fosters traditional free enterprise qualities. Through it, the owner of the diner
or the luncheonette gains a little advantage on his competition down
the block.

Or, parking violations—this man is feeding people and people
are double-parked in front of his store. Now you are not hurting
him, you are just helping the people who are buying things from
him, not that anyone else is involved. Yet it's looked at—because
you are a police officer—as corruption because the people are
parked out there. Now, who is actually going to get hurt now?
The people who are double parking, not the store owner. So in
fact you are not hurting the cop [by calling him corrupt] but
the store owner or the people who are going to buy something.
(25)

Even the common practice for police officers to make small money payments of $5 or $10 to the roll-call men in the precinct house in return for choice assignments or services rendered (choice of days off or vacation dates)[35] is rationalized by one respondent as a basic and respectable part of American business, usually called an expense account.

> The stuff this guy [Patrolman Droge] said on TV that the roll-call man makes money. The roll-call guy gets money for special assignments and stuff. In some houses [precincts] it is true, roll-call men will get money—$5 or $10 from patrolmen. It's like business I think. If you want a certain job and you can get it this way, why not? If guys want to work with a certain guy what's wrong with this? (In other words, you wouldn't consider this corruption?) No, that's my opinion. As I said it's only a job. Like I said, in business a boss has an expense account and he takes people out and chalks it up on the expense account. (18)

Our respondents believe that society has used the police officer as a scapegoat or "whipping boy" for its neurotic attitude toward corruption. In other words, the Knapp Commission is well aware that society offers the policeman bribes, yet it denounces *his* corruption. Our police ask how we can expect him to be a member of society, yet not share in its values. After all, policemen are simply like others who commit the same or worse acts. In short, the problem is not police corruption but a lawless society.

> The Knapp Commission is telling the policeman not to be corrupt in a corrupt society, which is impossible. It is impossible to be 100 percent legal. In other words, it is impossible to be absolutely legal when the society around you is illegal. That's what it all comes down to. (42)

This face-saving appeal supports another typical screen or defense against charges of police corruption—that is, to mask their own involvement, our respondents look for places to distribute the blame for police corruption, and this serves to protect them from being put on the spot. For example, uniformed patrolmen are considered spotless. Those making a killing are the top brass. It is difficult to tell whether our respondents are honest or simply resentful that they are not getting more. When they express resentment, they blame the bosses.

With respect to the Knapp Commission, everyone knows that corruption was there. We knew about it. So the Knapp Commission wasn't proving anything. And the people they really wanted to find, they didn't. That's all they did was to hit cops. They never hit bosses. And this is where the real money is lying. (25)

Police also complain that too little attention was paid to corruption in the Fire Department, the Sanitation Department, and in the upper reaches of city government. Why pick on the police? Even though the Knapp Commission stated in its final report that it had "neither the legal authority nor the financial resources to investigate other government agencies, much less society as a whole,"[36] our police object to being singled out.

There is corruption in the Police Department. There is corruption in the Housing Department. There are firemen who will steal your wallet on your bureau. I know this to be a fact. If there is a fire in a liquor store—well, God help the guy who owns the liquor store. Boy, what they take! Who can check up on these guys? . . . But we make news. Nobody else makes news. Housing inspectors don't make news. Cops make news. Corruption in the police makes news. Everything we do makes news. People like to read about cops. They can identify with cops. And they get their rocks off by seeing a cop get it. All right. But the point is that there is corruption all about us. (35)

It is probably true, as this respondent points out, that the police department is significantly not more corrupt than other city departments. But it is difficult today for politicians to protect the police or to be deliberately blind to corruption. Mayor Lindsay, for example, was not anxious to protect the police because of his commitment to blacks—the department became a "whipping boy" even though some of the accusations of corruption are true. Our respondents blame Lindsay for making corruption in the department a major issue. They believe Lindsay's interest in exposing police corruption was a political strategy to get large blocks of voters, notably blacks and Puerto Ricans.

A guy who becomes a cop fighter gets a reputation. Look at the balls of that guy—he's fighting cops. Cops are the lowest level, right? Now, look at the highest level. Look what Lindsay is doing to those cops. Look at the people who are taking on J. Edgar Hoover. Years ago you didn't take on J. Edgar Hoover. Now it's like a badge of courage. So do you follow me? This becomes an image thing. This was the good thing politically for Lindsay to do in New York. The policeman saw his big push on corruption just to get votes. . . . He couldn't give a shit about us. The only thing he cared about was his political career. John Lindsay is going to make it to the White House on the back of our graves. (27)

He kowtows to minorities which I think is totally wrong. First of all he is a minority mayor which might have a lot to do with it. And he has to be grateful to somebody somehow and this is probably his way of getting back at the majority. (29)

Other policemen feel that he was willing to pillory the police for corruption but was not willing to attack crime in the streets. Lindsay, it is argued, was just like any liberal who is more concerned over the rights of gangs and thugs than with the policeman's rights.

When a man turns around and calls me corrupt and then turns around and hands these fighting gangs in the Bronx a million dollars in poverty funds to open up storefronts and clubhouses and to buy guns. And this is a fact! I'll get up on television if I have the opportunity to say so. These fighting gangs are doing nothing but terrorizing the schools in the Bronx. They had a Kill Whitey Day last week. They put seventeen kids in the hospital.

I remember I looked out my window and there were about 200 Negroes and in the back of their jackets they had the Black Spades and Ghetto Brothers on the back of their coats. And they were in formation under my window screaming "Kill Whitey, Kill Whitey." (37)

Still others argue that the investigation into police corruption was a ploy to conceal scandals in the city administration.

It was timed to conceal the municipal loan and credit scandal. When this thing hit the newspapers and Postel [a city councilman] was making all those waves these hearings [Knapp Commission hearings] overrode it. What do they want to hear? They don't want to hear about somebody sitting in an office taking a few thousand or a couple of dozen. They don't want to hear this. They want to hear about the cop who is on the take for a deuce or a four or five dollar bill. They don't want to hear about politicians up there in office. There is no glamour—there is no excitement about politicians. But these politicians are making millions. But these guys are protected. They have laws to protect them. Who's on our side? Nobody! (20)

Former Commissioner Murphy also receives a good share of the blame for the issue of corruption. Our respondents are disgusted, bitter, and angry over his "blanket indictment" and "administrative innuendo" of the lack of integrity and efficiency of the police officer.

Well, really, all he has done is to make a lot of accusations. I mean, you know, I can't sit here to be honest with you and say there is no corruption. There is going to be corruption, but he is making a blanket indictment, and this is wrong. He said that the Narcotics Bureau was rampant with corruption. He should have locked up those guys instead of making a statement about the whole bureau. (16)

Other policemen believe that Commissioner Murphy was wrong to make corruption the number one priority of his administration.

They believe that Murphy's job was to enforce the law, fight crime, and defend the police against cop killings.

> Police officers get shot down in the street. Under his administration cops were being murdered—shot in the back! They had their own guns emptied into them! And what did he do? He held a five-minute commentary on that and a forty-five-minute commentary on police corruption. And if that didn't take every man on this job right by the throat and just choke him to death, I don't know what did. This hurt us more than anything else. . . . (20)

Murphy's efforts to restore discipline and maximum integrity by criticizing police complicity in the spreading drug traffic, and his attempts to root out an attitude that permits good police work to be undermined by corruption, is seen by our respondents as a systematic attempt to destroy the morale of the force.[37]

> We hate the man. We hate him quite intensely. (Why?) Because he is running scared with this integrity thing. He goes overboard. He is getting kind of hairy, so to speak. And he is destroying the moral of this department. (33)

The last striking example of a phobic screen or defense strategy appears when the police criticize the Knapp Commission for failure to adhere to strict principles of legality or to a code of deeds, propriety, and observances. Respondents use the language of legalisms to avoid the question of corruption, and to divest corruption of any personal meaning. Corruption is spoken of as a problem of legality or political theory. This device shows a concern with legal victories of righteousness, propagandizing, and rationalizing, not with the genuine problem of police corruption.

Using this strategy, our police complain that the Knapp proceedings were a "charade" or "Roman circus" conducted as an adversary trial or inquisition rather than as a judicial hearing. Furthermore, our police believe that their co-workers were badgered by the chief counsel (Michael F. Armstrong) and other hostile

members of the commission who were only interested in furthering
their political careers.

I feel that a good deal of the public resented what he done. He
turned around and he took a very responsible job and he made
a circus out of it. But by making a circus out of it he ruined the
morale of this job. And I felt that he was very reckless on a lot
of things that he did. And I don't think you do anything for
justice and the law and all the fine clichés to justify something
like that. And I think because of people like Mr. Armstrong this
is why we lose police powers. This is why we have Miranda.
This is why we have all those Supreme Court decisions. Because
you have some person in an investigative field who overex-
tended himself. . . . He did a pretty good job of demolishing the
image of this job—tarnishing it very much above and beyond
what it deserved. He also did a very good job of forcing resentment of that kind of investigative body. . . . Just like people
remember Joe McCarthy and his era. What is this? McCarthy-
ism, right? (27)

The greatest concern of our respondents is their belief that the
hearings violated their procedural and constitutional safeguards.
Evidence, most of which was illegally acquired through electronic
surveillance and unreliable informer testimony, was not subject to
cross-examination.

Not being able to cross-examine was the big thing. Lots of
people understood this, that they were not being cross-examined,
but they didn't care because they felt it was the truth, so who
cares? We don't really have civil rights. I found this out. I felt
that we were treated somewhat less than the lowest criminal.
(35)

Another officer continues in this vein:

It wasn't even a question of cross-examining that I felt was
wrong. All the questions were presented in a manner that no
court would permit. All the questions were led, like, "didn't you

at that time. . . ?" It was all staged. The only thing that was missing was the band and the choreography. (28)

Other respondents complain about the character of the credibility of rogue cops who turned informers for the commission. The testimony given by these "traitors to the uniform" confirms what our police believe to be the bogus nature of the whole Knapp Commission procedures and "proves" that the testimony of the witnesses was forced.

Until they got hold of Phillips and Waverly Logan and Droge, until they got a hold of these three individuals, they had nothing on the police force except sour grape allegations by citizens which they couldn't substantiate. . . . This guy Phillips owns three places, a real estate and a travel agency. You are going to tell me that he is not into a bit more? This guy must have been a real wheeler-dealer. Now for a man to be a thief for fourteen years and then to turn around and call every other man in the police force a thief, well, reason leads you to believe that the guy is just defending his position. (20)

If they had run an honest investigation, but take a look at all the witnesses. Phillips was a convicted cop, convicted by his own testimony. Waverly Logan, Droge—all of them admitted thieves—admitted "skanks" [a scornful term applied to criminals]. They sold their shields! And they will never be able to get back what they sold. (28)

It is important to remember that police have frequently compensated for their deficiencies in investigative work by using "stool pigeons" or informers who would keep detectives who protected them aware of criminal activities.[38] The nature of police work, and the opportunities it provides to cover up dishonesty (not to mention the "code of secrecy"), makes it difficult to get evidence in any other way. Like the professional thief, the corrupt cop tries to operate in circumstances in which he cannot be caught. Thus the use of police informers is a legitimate police strategy. This is recognized by one police officer.

> Every investigator has to use his informers. . . . So they got a
> guy like Phillips who is a dishonest guy from the start. They
> caught him with his hands in the till and then managed to use
> him after that like they would any informer. Every cop says,
> "Look at the bum you are using as a witness." But you don't
> get rabbis—you don't get priests who are involved in these sit-
> uations that you can normally use as witnesses. You get the
> bums. The DAs use informers who have long yellow sheets
> [arrest records] with past crimes they have committed. They
> have to use them. They put them on the stand and they say, "Tell
> the jury what you know." (32)

But our respondents also question the credibility of honest police
officers like Detective Frank Serpico. It will be recalled that Serpico
was the idealistic, independent crusader against police corruption
whose testimony of names and places was instrumental in bringing
about the Knapp Commission investigation.

> Well, is that guy [Serpico] legitimate? He is a guy, not that I
> am knocking anybody, who lives in the Village and he associates
> with all of his friends there. Let's face it, most of the people who
> live in the Village are ultraliberals. . . . So you wonder—is he a
> credible witness? . . . But they are playing him up. This is the
> guy who it telling us everybody is crooked. (16)

Our respondents conclude, then, that those who criticize them for
being corrupt fail to make allowances for the many social pressures,
contingencies, collusions, and compromises that oblige some policemen to break the law. They also assert that their critics have failed
to take into account individual differences among the police concerning their inclination to exploit the opportunities available to them.
Thus, from the police standpoint, a proper perspective on police
corruption must recognize how the web of social pressures and individual differences make strict compliance to police codes extremely
difficult.

Moreover, our police contend that continued exposure of police
corruption jeopardizes their methods of developing and maintaining

a corps of informers, and undermines their esprit de corps. Public exposure of police corruption creates disorder and anomie among the police. As individuals, the most they can do is to take refuge from the heat of the accusations and exposures in collective strategies, defenses, excuses, or justifications. They stubbornly defend themselves against charges of misconduct because they believe that they alone fully understand the problem of corruption and have the sole right to say what corruption is and when corrupt acts have been committed.

Yet regardless of individual responsibility, the burden of police corruption should be assumed by all police officers. The role of the police officer is so clear-cut that all his attempts to justify, excuse, or rationalize misconduct cannot shift the responsibility for corruption to society or to any other city agency or public official. No one stands closer to police corruption than the policeman.

Nevertheless, in his eyes, the white policeman's strong identification with "society" justifies his participation in corruption and bribery. He is following the lead of politicians and businessmen, and gaining economic rewards, even though these may not contribute to his social mobility. According to the policeman's understanding of his pact with society, exposure of corruption is one more betrayal by society and its leaders.

NOTES

1. See *The Knapp Commission Report on Police Corruption* (New York: George Braziller, 1972).

2. For a brief history of police corruption see David Burnham, "Some of Knapp Findings Have Ring of Historical Familiarity," *The New York Times*, August 7, 1972. For incidents of New York City police corruption at the turn of the century see Emanuel H. Lavine, *Secrets of The Metropolitan Police* (New York: Garden City Publishing Co., 1937).

3. See "Report Says Police Corruption in 1971 Involved Well Over Half on the Force," *The New York Times*, December 28, 1972.

4. *Knapp Commission Report*, op. cit., pp. 7–8. Also see Fred J. Cook, "How Many Rotten Apples in the Barrel?" *The New York Times*, October 24, 1971.

5. See Juan M. Vasques, "40 Indictments Expected as Result of Knapp Data," *The New York Times*, October 15, 1971.

6. *Knapp Commission Report,* op. cit., p. 35.

7. Ibid., pp. 35–41; also Exhibit 7, p. 282.

8. As reported by David Burnham, "Knapp Unit Faults Mayor on Corruption of Police," *The New York Times,* July 2, 1971; and David Burnham, "Knapp Panel says Walsh and Others Ignored Tips by U.S. on Police Crimes," *The New York Times,* December 28, 1972.

9. *Knapp Commission Report,* op cit., p. 41. See also David Burnham, "Policeman Tells of Unit's Graft," *The New York Times,* May 11, 1971.

10. As reported by David Burnham, "Knapp Unit Faults Mayor on Corruption of Police," *The New York Times,* July 2, 1971.

11. As reported by Clark Whelton, "From Free Apples to Pusher Pay-Offs," *The Village Voice,* June 10, 1971.

12. See, for example, David Burnham, "Murphy to Shift Jobs of 200 Today," *The New York Times,* May 21, 1971; Will Lissner, "Murphy Cautions Top-Level Aides a Shake-up Is Due," *The New York Times,* August 23, 1971; David Burnham, "Murphy to Check on Aides' Finances," *The New York Times,* August 24, 1971; Michael Knight, "Murphy to Transfer 30 from Harlem," *The New York Times,* August 25, 1971; David Burnham, "Murphy Promotes an Inspector for Fighting Police Corruption," *The New York Times,* August 28, 1971; David Burnham, "Murphy Relieves 6 Police Captains for Laxity on Job," *The New York Times,* September 1, 1971; David Burnham, "Police Sergeants Told to Be Tough," *The New York Times,* September 4, 1971.

13. *Knapp Commission Report,* op. cit., Exhibit 4, Interim Report of Investigative Phase, pp. 273–276.

14. See editorial, "Cooping of a Sort," *The New York Times,* September 4, 1971.

15. As reported by David Burnham, "Police Captains Denounce Inquiry," *The New York Times,* August 3, 1971.

16. As reported by Walter H. Waggoner, "Police Sergeants Union Seeks to Bar Hearings by Knapp Group," *The New York Times,* October 14, 1971.

17. For a slightly different discussion of these terms see *Knapp Commission Report,* op. cit., pp. 65–66.

18. Ibid., pp. 65–66.

19. Ibid., pp. 89, 170–182.

20. See David Burnham, "Lindsay Defends Knapp Hearings," *The New York Times,* October 26, 1971; also, "Excerpts from Mayor's Statement on Knapp Panel," *The New York Times,* August 29, 1972.

21. See David Burnham, "Lindsay Praises Gains by Murphy," *The New York Times,* July 23, 1971.

22. As reported by David Burnham, "P.B.A. Head Says Murphy Is Destroying Police Force," *The New York Times,* September 3, 1971.

23. *Knapp Commission Report,* op. cit., p. 3.

24. Patrolman William R. Phillips, the principal witness, was described by the

President of the P.B.A. as a "liar, a burglar, a thief, a conniver, and a thoroughly rotten man." As reported by David Sellinger, "City Keeps Mum on Knapp Files," *The New York Post*, December 29, 1972.

25. See "Civil Liberties Unit Sees Knapp Inquiry as Violating Rights," *The New York Times*, October 23, 1971. Walter Knapp's reply to the charges appear in James F. Clarity, "Knapp Unit's Head Defends Legality of Investigation," *The New York Times*, October 24, 1971.

26. I draw upon *Knapp Commission Report*, op. cit., pp. 67–68.

27. See Jonathan Rubinstein, *City Police* (New York: Ballantine Books, 1973), pp. 402–403.

28. For a discussion of how these strategies are used as "excuses" and "justifications" see Standford M. Lyman and Marvin B. Scott, *A Sociology of the Absurd* (New York: Appleton-Century-Crofts, 1970), pp. 113–124.

29. Suggested in Erving Goffman, *Relations in Public* (New York: Basic Books, 1971), Part I, Chapter 6, "Normal Appearances," especially pp. 262–263.

30. Ibid., especially pp. 270, 278.

31. The term is borrowed from David Reisman, *Faces in the Crowd: Individual Studies in Character and Politics* (New Haven: Yale University Press, 1952).

32. Suggested in the Foreword to *Knapp Commission Report*, op. cit.

33. Ibid.

34. Ibid., pp. 170–182.

35. This practice is discussed at length in *Knapp Commission Report*, op. cit., pp. 166–169.

36. Ibid., Forword.

37. The general view among police today is that the present police commissioner (Michael Joseph Codd) has disappointed those men who had "anticipated a return to a more permissive attitude towards corruption, discipline," and accountability. See Selwyn Raab, "Codd Keeps Force Taut, If Not Wholly Happy," *The New York Times*, January 10, 1975. Codd's predecessor, Donald F. Cawley, was also criticized by the police for continuing Murphy's policies of "vigorous anti-corruption activities." See Robert D. McFadden, "Cawley to Press Graft Detection," *The New York Times*, August 24, 1973; also, Emanuel Perlmutter, "All Police Above Captain Will Face Annual Review," *The New York Times*, August 23, 1973.

38. See Nicholas M. Horrock, "Informers Play Key Police Role," *The New York Times*, April 2, 1975. For a thorough treatment of the use of informers see Malachi L. Harvey and John C. Cross, *The Informer in Law Enforcement*, 2d ed. (Springfield, Ill.: Charles C Thomas, 1968).

5

The White Policeman as Victim
of His Occupational World

This chapter deals with the effects of society's betrayal on the policeman's conception of himself as a useful and respectable member of the community. The white policeman believes that public respect for him has decreased and that concern for his well-being is negligible. He is told every day by word or attitude that he is a "pig" or worse. When his authority is challenged as he attempts to rectify breeches of order committed in his presence he concludes that respect for authority has disappeared. He is frequently abused, harassed, and shot at, and may even be murdered in the performance of his duties. At the same time, he believes that he has been sacrificed to the criminal element and lawlessness; courts, lawmakers, and press are thought to be callous to his needs and grievances. It is understandable then that he views the public with suspicion, as the embodiment of everything that is alien to his values, and, not infrequently, as an enemy.

To the extent that they have accepted the attitudes and language of their devaluation, policemen see themselves as victims of persecution. This common occupational outlook leads a substantial number, and perhaps a majority, of police officers to feel extreme discontent with their occupation.

In my study of black policemen the view of policemen as victims for whom the public has contempt was a persistent and common theme. Blacks in the ghetto identified the police as an instrument through which injustice was imposed and sustained. Police presence was considered symbolic of ghetto imprisonment, discrimination, and segregation. Black youth presented the black officer with special problems beyond those associated with vandalism or petty offenses or serious delinquencies. They taunted him with the charge that he was an Uncle Tom representing white power and the entire system of confinement in the ghetto.[1]

When I interviewed white policemen this theme of persecution was presented in terms of the Knapp Commission disclosures. All police respondents felt that the Knapp Commission hearings exacerbated anticop attitudes. Many respondents felt that the Knapp hearings did more than any other event in the history of the Police Department to destroy public trust in the police, supplanting Lindsay's request for a Civilian Police Review Board as the chief cause of making them scapegoats for the ills of society. Depending on the time of the interviews, then, there is a shift in focus. Essentially the same argument is made, but the adversary or enemy of the police changes.

The police, as our findings indicate, authenticate this image of persecution. They find it in the press. They find it in the courts. They find it in the mayor's office. They find it in the lack of respect with which they are treated on their beats, and they find it in the insolence with which they are treated by potential and actual criminals, especially by youth, and most extremely by black youth. They also find it in the radicalism that is part of the upper-middle class world, they find it in the lack of esteem with which they are held by friends and some family members. With their immediate family members they experience this most sharply. The stigma of being a cop is visited not only on themselves but on all they love and cherish. In all these cases, the white policeman finds himself totally alienated from and betrayed by his society.

THE DECLINE AND FALL OF THE POLICE REPUTATION. Many people complain about the police; many also praise them and commend their work. Yet only five policemen in this study believe that people are appreciative of police work. The majority believe that they lack respect and public recognition. This belief is held in spite of the thousands of unsolicited letters received annually by the Police Department commending police efficiency or describing the laudatory behavior of a particular police officer.[2] Through its Public Relations Unit, the Police Department makes these letters of commendation available to the rank and file in a monthly magazine, and no monthly report of complaints is published. Yet few respondents were willing to balance the negative public view with the positive, the complaints with the compliments. Apparently a segment of the public has a more favorable image of the police than the police have of themselves.

Interviews with our respondents brought forth a wide range of characterizations of their role to support their contention that nobody likes them.

> The job has definitely been downgraded. It had so much prestige. It's amazing when you think about it . . . how much prestige the job has lost over time. I remember when I went to parties and affairs, they used to say I was a policeman, as if the job was important to them. There was a great deal more respect. I can't wait to get out. There are so many people, including the law-abiding, who think and feel such terrible things about the policeman. When I'm in civilian clothes overhearing people talking about policemen saying that policemen are "pigs" or "fascist" or "gestapo" it makes me sick. (3)

> The police officer has become a target instead of a preventer or whatever you want to call it. He is no longer carrying the badge of Mr. Good Guy in the eyes of the people he deals with in those situations. Now he is just another object to throw a stone at or fire a shot at or throw a fire bomb at. It's not like it used to be. (20)

One officer assigned to Harlem describes the intensity of anti-police hostility that exists there.

Nobody likes you in Harlem. And I'm not the only cop who feels that way. They rag-mouth you. They will say anything. They know they can get away with it. It doesn't bother me though. Just don't hurt me, that's all. And I've lost a lot of respect for the black people up there. Maybe it's justifiable up there to have that feeling as a white cop. But any cop, white or black, would have problems. A friend of mine was shot on Lenox Avenue. He was shot twice. And he was shot for no reason at all. It was Saturday morning. There was about twenty-five people around. There were four garbagemen, four garbagemen right around the corner on their trucks. After this happened they all got on their trucks and left. (They left the cop there?) Yeah. They left him there. . . . What I'm getting at is that nobody wanted to come forward to help this cop or be a witness. Nobody saw anything. You get the feeling that nobody gives a shit for you when you're there. . . . (30)

Another Harlem-based officer tells us that antiwhite police prejudice is so extreme that blacks would rather not have white cops working there at all.

A call came over one night on the radio car that they wanted an ambulance. A lady's son was very sick and she would not let policemen into her house because they were white and she was black. They wanted a black policeman, plus a black ambulance attendant to come. Now this brings up two things: the public doesn't want you, and in this case, this person doesn't want you because you are white. We are helping her and yet she still rejects us. (22)

Then there is the insolence of black youth.

Out in Brooklyn, forget it. Black kids have never respected us anyway. They call you a pig and a motherfucker. This is not something new. (38)

They see you in a car and they call you a motherfucker and spit
at the car. If I get out of the car it would be an incident, so I
stay in the car. Sometimes I might say, "Do you know me to
call me that?" (23)

But the most humiliating attitude that the police officer must contend with is the view that he is a thief, an attitude that even people
of tolerance and goodwill toward the police currently share.

You are looked down upon more. People at one time might
have treated you as a person. Now there is much less of that
because they will look at you and right away say, "See that guy
over there—he's a thief! He sells narcotics to kids." And a good
portion of the public thinks like this. (25)

THE MORTIFICATION OF THE POLICE SELF

The Knapp Commission Is the Villain.   Many police officers hold
the Knapp Commission responsible for intensifying public indignation and engineering the attitude that "all policemen are a bad lot."
They also believe that the commission was insensitive to the probability that the honest police officer would suffer from the transgres-
sions of "the few." Thus the Knapp Commission bears the brunt for
perverting and belittling the police reputation. This is cause for extreme mortification.

(Is there any group that is sympathetic to the policeman today?) Not after the Knapp Commission. . . . I don't think we
will ever come back in the eyes of the public that we were six
or seven years ago. If there would be a way, I would be a one-
man missionary force, and I believe that 32,000 other guys
would be too, to try and right this. But I think the damage has
been done. They painted the department with one big brush and
said everyone is a thief. And this is absolutely wrong. Some of
the finest men I know are police officers. (26)

The Knapp Commission has inflicted the police officer with a sense

of persecution, making him feel insecure, defensive, and threatened
in his relations with the many individuals and groups that he routinely meets or confronts during a tour of duty. Police officers are
now extremely quick to detect real and imagined affronts to their
personal dignity.

For example, policemen believe that public indignation and increased internal police supervision fanned by the Knapp Commission hearings has damaged the good relationship they once had with
store owners. Store owners are now described as suspicious of police
presence, and rude or simply reluctant to accept their good company.
The police officer cannot count on their sympathy. The following
excerpt from a long interview makes this clear.

> If you go into a store for a glass of water and you stay in there
> for a little bit the public wants to know what you are doing.
> And there is all sorts of supervision, plus your own conscience.
> You know you can't just go into stores and stay there today.
> . . . You are afraid that the IAD is going to get the idea that
> you are going into the store to look for a favor or a discount
> or something that you want to buy. . . . I think years ago people
> were very glad to see a cop come into the store. They weren't
> even reluctant, they welcomed you. It wasn't even in their mind
> that you were trying to gain something. You were there to be
> friendly because you worked in the neighborhood. Your job was
> to protect the public and enforce the law. It's hard to find people
> like that today. They figure you want something for nothing.
> . . . You come into the store and he gives you a dirty look or
> he kind of ignores you. (21)

Consternation is especially aroused by the treatment policemen
receive at the hands of working-class youth of Irish extraction. The
Knapp Commission exposures have allegedly furnished even these
young people with a motive to goad or embarrass policemen. And
there is little he can do about it. Attempts to manipulate these youth
through appeals to idealism meet with failure because they can see
through it.

And then we have the lower half of the precinct, the Irish kids who are a little more outgoing, a little more vociferous, and they give us the same kind of crap. And there was a cop's son giving me that crap one day. (A cop's son?) Yeah. I guess he wanted to impress his friends in the eyes of the crowd. This is what you find today. And the Knapp Commission put it right on television just before the kiddie show. It's a wonder they didn't show it five times. When my daughter usually watches "Sesame Street" the Knapp Commission was on TV telling everybody how corrupt we are. What do you say to a kid who hears this stuff? It's like being a saint—the more you protest the crazier you look. (38)

The policeman also faces the accusations of the upper-middle-class, whose children may be less reluctant than their parents to express their negative image of the cop.

Every once in a while you get that snide remark. . . . You get it from the kids. The kids hear it. They hear it from home. And while the parents may be reluctant to say it to your face, the kids have absolutely no reluctance to tell you how they feel. A kid will come up and say, "How much money did you make today?" This is not uncommon. (Who are these kids?) They are upper-middle-class or upper-class kids. They will come up and tell you—and I have had it happen to me while I was standing on the corner, "Hey, Pig Crook!" These are little white kids, apparently Jewish, you know, a nice kid from a good home; and this nice Jewish kid comes up to me and says "Pig!" And I tell them, " Is this the way you were taught to talk?" For Christ's sake! And this is the kind of crap you run into. And you start to get the message after awhile. (38)

Finally, the Knapp Commission aroused the prejudice of the policeman's family and circle of friends. Their views are expressed through innuendo, humor, and furtive gesture, if not by direct accusations.

I have had people say to me, "How much graft have you been
taking lately?" And I have had friends of mine, and I have had
relatives of mine say to me, "How is the pad in the Youth Division?" (Relatives have said this to you?) Yes, relatives. They
said it in a joking manner. I hear it from friends of mine in the
line of work and I will ignore it completely. . . . I have heard
jokes like, "You are never around when we need you, but if
there is something to give you, like a free meal, you will always
be there." I have had many friends of mine who are the biggest
cop buffs in the whole world say things to me. I'm a great tease.
I'm a great kidder myself. And they will say it jokingly. But it's
there. And everybody is doing it. But after awhile it becomes
tiresome. (26)

The policemen pick up these masked attitudes quickly and learn
also to judge their significance no matter how they are concealed.
They deflate their sense of rightness and high virtue by forcing on
them a less flattering self-image. Long-time friendships may suffer.

A lot of my friends would say things to me in half-jest and half
maybe believing that things were going on. (What did they
say?) Things like money. Like, "Gee, I didn't know you were
making that kind of money." And it hurt me. And I didn't talk
to some of my friends specifically because of that. . . . (34)

Another officer describes a similiar situation but responds to it in a
defensive-aggressive way.

My friends would say half kiddingly that I was making $3000
a year under the table and stuff like that. . . . The plumber, who
I know quite well, makes some snide comment about how "all
cops are on the take." And I tell him about all the money he
has made by overcharging us. Who is the real thief? (36)

Another officer describes the heavy-handed sarcasm directed against
him by the patrons of a neighborhood bar.

Even after work where you might go to a bar and somebody is

sitting there and they know you are a cop and they really break
your chops. (What do they say?) They say, "Why don't they
buy? They've got plenty of money." (18)

In self-defense, policemen joke among themselves about these
incidents.

When you go to work everybody talks about it. Of course, you've
got to talk about it. They make jokes about it. One cop says he
is going to make out a big sign and put it on his radio car:
THIS CAR DOES NOT ACCEPT MONEY OR OTHER GRATUITIES—
PLEASE STAY AWAY. (18)

A police officer whose transfer within the department coincided
with the Knapp hearings describes the "sly innuendo" he receives
from people in his neighborhood.

A week later I was in the 77th precinct, from the Bronx to
Brooklyn. So, as I said, when I got transferred out there the
people on the block, and even my own family, started to ask
me what went wrong. There was sly little innuendo. In other
words, they believed I screwed up somewhere. I got caught with
my hand in the till. But nothing of the sort happened. But just
because of the simple fact that I got transferred, when all of
this bullshit was going on, everybody said, "Gee, he's doing
something wrong." And you feel like a schmuck in your own
neighborhood. You are walking around like an idiot. It's a funny
thing because everybody looked at you like you were a criminal.
(38)

Neighbors' attitudes may also be mirrored in nonverbal gestures.
One police officer describes a common furtive gesture used by policemen to signify corruption. When used by neighbors or outsiders with
respect to policemen, however, the gesture takes on the character of
personal derogation, belittling distrust, and is greatly resented.

I bought a new car. I'm thirty-five years old and this is my first
full-sized car. It's a Chevy, right? I got air conditioning in it.

I'm in hock up to my ears with this—with the miserable credit unions. But I had to buy a new car. We have three kids and that Cross Bronx Expressway is a horror without air conditioning. I also have a Volkswagen, okay. But I have a Volkswagen because I've totaled [demolished] two Volkswagens in the past two years. And I collected for it. I got money for it! Now, there is an old gesture. When a person asks you, "How are you?" (respondent puts his palm out directly in back of him)—when a cop does this it's a joke as a sign of graft. Anyway, our neighbor says, "I see you got a new car." And then she gives this gesture to my wife. Now, my wife didn't know what it meant. She is rather naive. She told me about this, and that it had taken place. And I got a little bit angry. They may have meant it as a joke. Cops do this with other cops. They kid around this way. They do it knowing full well it is an in-joke. But when she did it, well, it got me mad. (35)

Even a policeman's wife may become suspicious.

My wife wanted to know why I am working as an exterminator if we are making all this money like Knapp said we are. (36)

Another policeman's sister-in-law is merciless on this issue, and he hotly resents her accusations.

As a matter of fact my own family was asking me, "What did you do? What went wrong?" (Are you serious?) God is my judge. My sister-in-law, to show you blatant hypocrisy, she called me one day. She calls my wife often, and she asks me what I think of the Knapp hearings. And I said, "Well, it shouldn't be publicized." Just what I told you. And she says, "Well, I think it should. I think you guys are getting away with an awful lot." Now this is my sister-in-law talking. So I said, "Well, if you feel that way, fine," so I give the phone to my wife. Do you know she called me up two weeks later and she wants a Christmas tree—wanted me to get her a tree on the arm [for free]? (18)

Such incidents make it clear that many policemen may suffer for "the indiscretions of the few." A certain cynicism and hardness is bound to result.

A Bad Cop Makes Good News. The press also receives blame for the public's low opinion of policemen. Police officers have long expected the press to emphasize the punitive nature of their role rather than the social services they provide. Our respondents contend that they handle family quarrels, personal disputes, fires, and give medical services to the sick. They see it as a part of their job to serve as medical experts, social workers, lawyers, psychiatrists, and priests. Needless to say, these multifaceted roles require strength, skill, courage, restraint, and impartiality. No other professional group performs such a variety of services on a round-the-clock demand. Yet the press seems irresistably drawn to the negative, the sensational, and the tawdry aspects of the policeman's job.

Well, first of all, positive things don't make news. Who cares about the positive? Who cares about the cop who helped a sick person, or picked up a drunk or an injured person off the street? They photograph firemen putting their mouths on babies' mouths. We do it all day long. We can get spinal meningitis as far as we know. The press is simply interested when someone is entrusted with a public trust and betrays that trust. Not when he holds that trust in good stead. . . . (33)

The bad press is part of the reality the police officer lives with:

The Police Department will never have a good press. We are a punitive agency. We don't deal in a positive nature of things. Our job is always viewed in a negative way. . . . (20)

The press is also charged with sensationalizing police corruption and other forms of police misbehavior. By so doing, it prejudices the public against the police, and perverts the high ideals of the best police officers.

Well, no matter what happens it seems as if they knock the cops. It never has anything good to say. Once in a while you get a good story. But most of the time they have something degrading to say about the cop. If a cop gets locked up or if there is corruption in the department as it has so well been publicized. It really annoys you because with 32,000 men there is going to be incidents. There are going to be things wrong or something is going to happen. Can you imagine having a corporation with 32,000 people in it, and the head of it gets caught and they publicize that the entire corporation is corrupt? How can they do that? But that is what they are doing. (18)

Journalistic ethics require the press to report activities of the state accurately. If the press calls attention to police corruption, it must do so by presenting accurate facts and enlightened comment.[3] This is precisely what our respondents feel the press is not doing. They believe that police corruption is sensationalized and made the basis of appeal to the public because reporters, publishers and managing editors have as their primary goal a desire to attract attention— that is, to give the public what they think the public wants to hear.

Policemen also criticize the source of newspaper information, often accusing reporters of inaccuracy and exaggeration in police stories. Policemen feel that reporters are so biased that they present a distorted and even fabricated picture of police life. Seldom does a reporter interview the police officer directly involved in a case. Reporters are seen as exploiters of rumor, suspicion, and inference. It is no wonder, then, that our respondents are demoralized by what they consider a "lawless" press.

The news media knows all the problems. They will listen to everybody and his brother, except the police. If you have something to say, they'll print it. It doesn't matter how much validity is involved in this statement that is made. If a police officer was involved in a very ticklish situation, and he was there and observed it, he should know what happened. But let the news media report it. Well, it's not written the way you say it. And you were there! You observed it! . . . It's amazing what they do with stories. . . . (What do you think is the cause for this distortion in the news media?) I feel these writers today write exactly as they want to write. In other words, they are doing their own thing. And these people who read it enjoy the writings of one person, let's say. Now for myself, I enjoy Dick Young. And he also answers other questions other than sports. But I feel he is straight and to the point. Now Pete Hamill, I think who writes for the *Post*, well, I don't think he helps the situation too much. I don't mind anyone, as long as they call a spade a spade. (15)

Our police recognize the subjective influences on reporters, and bitterly criticize how subjectivism has "poisoned" reporters' views of police news. They may even develop a personal vendetta against particular reporters who have damaged the police image.

Gabe Pressman was involved in a riot in 1964. And he was involved in a situation where he ended up in back of a police van. And a number of prisoners done a number on him. He was being beat up by prisoners. He was in the back of a van with black prisoners and he was screaming inside, and the police officers were, let us say, not making an energetic effort to get him out of there. Show me a man who hates a cop more and I'll show you another Pete Hamill. This guy is unbelievably biased and prejudiced against cops. Between Hamill and Gabe Pressman, I don't know how we have survived in the press. Jimmy Breslin, well, forget it. He's got people on the job in his family —did you know that? But they are "pigs," Breslin says. Anyone who will have a beer with this fellow now is out of their skull if they are on this job. It's got to be sensationalism when they write this stuff. It sells newspapers. Besides, I never met an objective reporter in my life. There is always a slight bias no matter who it is. To the right or the left there is always a personal bias. Take this guy Rivera on Channel 7. He's a Puerto Rican fellow. I had that guy in court because one of his relatives got locked up and he was trying to use his influence as a reporter to help the situation. He was peddling influence. He was name-dropping all over court. He sat down and we were holding a conversation. Mr. Nice Guy! He tells us, "Gee you guys do a good job." I told him I wish he would get on the air and say that. "Why don't you get on television and say that?" No, they won't do that. It's always the negative. . . . (20)

POLICE ARE SCAPEGOATS FOR THE INCREASE IN CRIME. Most of the policemen in this study (thirty-six out of forty respondents queried) believe that crime in the city has continued to rise despite attempts by city politicians and precinct commanders to manipulate crime statistics through "new methods" of reporting crime and statistical "gimmickery" that understates certain violent crimes.[4]

Oh, yeah. Well, we hear the FBI reports and they say it's on the increase. I also feel this by just listening to the patrol car radio. And if you work for a precinct long enough, you will find that crime is increasing. (38)

Oh, sure. Crime is going up. I think this precinct is an example. We are making more arrests than ever in this precinct. I think crime is spreading to all over the city. (16)

Even the attempt by the Police Department to "downgrade" serious crimes by creating a false reduction in the city's major crime rate does not alter the common police view that crime is on the rise.

There was a time when you reported a crime if a man was knocked down on the street—the forcible taking of property, in this case, was a robbery. The surest statute in the book is robbery. But if he wasn't hurt and there were no witnesses you could make it larceny. You could make it a grand larceny which is not a crime against the person but more of a crime against property. So they just changed it around because robbery is a more serious crime. But that's playing with statistics. (31)

Even though fighting street crime has always been the first priority of police, and the absence of crime the best proof of police efficiency, police officers believe that they have little effect on the crime rate, and deeply resent the common tendency to blame them for the rise in crime. At best, the Police Department as a preventive agency displaces crime by pushing it from certain precincts or neighborhoods into adjoining areas.[5] Moreover, crimes that usually occur indoors (like burglaries and felonious assaults) are apparently unaffected by police presence. The department has more men out on the streets than ever before. It has sent most of its men to high crime areas and has modernized its equipment. Nevertheless, reported crime in the city has continued to rise.[6]

All uniformed police officers would probably like to believe that they are a deterrent to crime, but many reluctantly admit that they are not.

> The police officer is supposed to be a deterrent. That's why he is out there. But apparently it doesn't work that way, at least among ghetto residents. (22)

Police presence does not suppress crime, it simply displaces it to an adjoining area.

> In other words, the perpetrator will say, "I am not going to hold up a shoe store where I see the cop," but maybe he will go to another store around the corner, a five and dime store, and will hold that one up. (15)

A few officers believe that in the case of spur-of-the-moment crimes, where the offender is not a hardened criminal, the uniform does not even displace crime.

> No, they don't give a shit about you. In fact, I walked to my old neighborhood and I walked into a candy store to buy a pack of cigarettes. There are two guys that I know, they are younger than me. I knew them when they were eight years old and now they are junkies. And there was a cop on foot patrol standing on the corner talking to a woman, and these guys started to fight right in front of the cop. They were breaking up the store. They

didn't care. . . . When I was a kid I would never think of starting a fight with a cop there. Some of them just don't give a
damn. (14)

Blacks Live a Life of Crime. Crime is a multi-faceted problem;
little is known about it and how to fight it.[7] William H.
Parker, for-
mer Commissioner of the Los Angeles Police Department, is probably
close to the truth when he says that the only thing that can be said
with any degree of assurance about crime rates is that they "rise and
fall on the tides of economic, social, and political cycles with em-
barrassingly little attention to the most determined efforts of our
police."[8]

But although policemen deeply resent the common practice of the
public to make them scapegoats for the increase in crime, an all-too-
common reaction of the police is to find another scapegoat—the
blacks. Police officers not only believe that most crimes are committed by blacks, but also that any attempt to solve black violence
and crime must come from police repression of blacks rather than
from attempts to solve the economic, social, and racial problems facing many blacks. This belief persists despite evidence that crime
rates have increased in industrialized societies that include few or no
blacks.

Here are replies to the question, Who are the people committing
all this crime?

Well, the majority of them, I don't want to sound like a racist
or anything, are the minorities. I think you can see that just by
the prison population. You know, like they said, look at Attica,
it's all Negroes. You know, there was eighty percent there. (16)

Most of the crime is done by blacks. You go to Riker's Island
[a prison] and that's all you can see. You see very few whites,
and the white guys you do see are drifters or kids stealing cars.
But ninety percent of them are black or Puerto Rican, but
mostly black. (29)

A few respondents attribute the high crime rate among blacks to fixed racial inheritance, to moral degeneracy, to lack of family life, and to idleness that encourages violence.

> Blacks have more rights than they ever had and they want more. They don't want to be equal to whites, they want to be superior to whites! They want to reverse positions with whites—that's all they want. Blacks are a different breed of people, the way they think. They have no family life. They are screwing everybody here and there. Most colored guys have no identification. They may call themselves Jones but their mother's name is Williams, and their father's name, if they know him or have a father, is something else. There is no one supervising them. They want to do things for kicks. And they want more and they don't want to work and it's easier to steal. They love to commit crime. They love it. They love to stick a knife into you. They have a revenge for doing this and they get money for it, too. They are ruthless people. (23)

The majority of the respondents are more moderate and conciliatory in their tone, and modulate their racial attitudes if, and when, they express them. Nevertheless, they too have reached the decision that blacks are responsible for the high incidence of antisocial and criminal acts in the racial ghetto, and that the police have no influence or control over them.

> I guess it comes from the upbringing of people and the type of area they live in and things that have been going around in their neighborhood. You take a neighborhood like Harlem. You expect the people to act as the neighborhood is. Some do and some don't. I grew up in Brownsville, which is not too good a neighborhood. But I am a police officer. I went from one extreme to another. . . . So it all depends on the person. If he is strong enough he will not be affected by his environment. I believe it all has to do with motivation to overcome the surroundings. Too many people put emphasis on the neighborhood the person comes from and blame the neighborhood. In other words, they don't want to put the blame on themselves. (25)

A Permissive and Overlegalized Society. As we have seen, our respondents bemoan their ineffectiveness in reducing crime. One contributing factor is seen as a soft, permissive, overlegalized society.[9] The emphasis on civil rights and privileges, they say, has been so distorted by liberals and misguided judges that it has led to license and anarchy. Restrictions on police interrogation and court decisions on search and seizures have removed an effective deterrent to crime. And we are paying an exhorbitant price for these changed attitudes —increased crime and diminished law enforcement.

> In our society today the hypocrisy of the whole liberal movement in this country is a cause of our feelings of frustration and anger. It seems that the cradle of the whole liberal movement in this country is to forgive and forget. There always has to be an excuse for some wrongdoing under the guise of freedom of expression. There has to be some excuse for a rapist, a murderer, a junky, a protester. We are all born in this world to carry a cross. But it seems that the liberal was born to save the world. This is a hypocritical fallacy. The doors are always opened to the criminal. But when it comes to the police they slam the door in our face. When you make a mistake your name is given to the newspapers, your wife's name, your child's name. You are also put in the position of being disgraced. This is some contrast! ... (13)

The most discouraging aspect of police work is felt to be the ease with which the average citizen has accepted the steady rise in lawlessness and the loss of police protection.

> It's getting to the point where mugging is becoming acceptable as a way of life. Where you accept your car being vandalized, ruined, or where your new car will be stolen. The public has accepted these crimes—where criminals can get away with anything—in fact, they are encouraged. Our standards in this country have become so loose that rape, the violation of our body, has even become acceptable, not to say anything of property. How do we make people aware of what is going on? (13)

The police respond by demanding that the state give them back the powers taken from them by federal court decisions. They believe that policing the modern city requires broad, flexible, discretionary police powers to deal not only with violent crimes committed by blacks, but also with the annoying conduct of young middle-class and upper-class drug users and protesters. Only then do they feel they can concentrate on protecting the innocent.

Moreover, respondents believe they have been crippled by constitutional law to fit into the liberals' vision of society. On this issue, they focus their attacks on the Lindsay Administration.

You are beating your head against the brick wall. You are not going to stop this permissiveness. This is going to have to come from the Lindsay Administration. They are going to have to turn the cops out there and let them do a job. *Do the job!* If you are out there and somebody gives you a hard time, use force. But this is not the policy. The policy is, be out there but don't create waves. Now all of this works on the innards of the man. One of the things that turned my stomach was that rally at City Hall when the animals jumped all over the patrol cars, and all the vandalism down there. Nothing was done about it. Nothing has been done about the riots, the small riots that we have down on the streets everyday. Sanitation doesn't pick up the garbage so they turn over the garbage and start fires. There is anarchy on the streets of New York today. And we can thank Mayor Lindsay for it. (15)

At one time, policemen stressed the idea that the city's black crime rate would decrease if Lindsay would stop interfering with police actions, and would discontinue his policy of appeasing blacks and their organizations to further his own political ambitions.

Then our liberal mayor has made it possible for any organization of people to walk all over the Police Department. You lock up a colored person and the first thing that happens is that you locked him up because he was black. And right off the bat you are prejudiced. The colored person calls up his organization to complain against you. And Lindsay encourages this. Or, if some black guy comes at you with something we are told to wait until he hits you. That is, we are told to hold back as much as we can. This is something that ten years ago, if you just looked at cop in the wrong way he would give you a rap in the back of your head and send you flying. You can't do this today. If the cop had more freedom to do what he wanted to do you wouldn't have so much crime in the streets as you do now. And I think we owe this to our mayor who gave the NAACP or any one of these organizations all the power to do whatever they want, and to do it whenever they want. And the only reason he does this is politics—that is, to get the support of the colored, he kowtows to them, you know, he is a white brother. (25)

THE POLICE ARE HAMSTRUNG BY THE COURTS. The police officer gets rewards and satisfaction from the arrests he makes, and thus, satisfaction that he is reducing crime. But because this satisfaction can only be confirmed through prosecution, conviction, and sentencing, any failure or interference with this sequence is experienced by the police as self-defeating and demoralizing. If the courts abrogate their responsibility to support the police, then the law, the courts, and the judges become the enemies of the police.[10]

The most common police criticism of the criminal justice system is that an officer too often sees the charges that he made on a legitimate "collar" being reduced through plea bargaining or thrown out. As a result, criminals with long police records are out on bail or parole ("cut loose") committing further crimes.[11]

I had a narcotics pusher that I arrested . . . and this guy went before the grand jury. . . . He was indicted and went up to Part 35 of the Supreme Court for trial. And it turned out that he was permitted by a judge to plead guilty to criminal possession of a dangerous drug and he was sentenced to the time already served in jail, which was twenty-nine days! Now, this, to me, doesn't aspire any great hope in the cop who makes an arrest. (28)

This respondent goes on to describe the system in terms of adversaries litigating disputed facts and points of law while a judge decides who is right. But he believes the inevitable result is reduced sentences for the criminal.

Very few of them go to trial in the courts today. Everything is a deal. They stand right there in front of the judge, and the arresting officer making the complaint as a witness, and they say, "Mr DA, if my client would plead guilty to attempted petty larceny?" The DA will say, "No, he's got a strong sheet [long arrest record] here now. He's been arrested quite a few times. We are going to hold out for an attempted grand larceny." Then the defense attorney says, "We won't take a felony under any conditions. Give us another misdemeanor." And they are charging the guy with the attempt to commit a crime that couldn't have taken place outside of the Artic—that is, the attempted rape of a polar bear. The guy was originally charged with grand larceny of an automobile. But they don't care what he pleads guilty to as long as the DA gets a guilty plea and defense counsel can get him off on a misdemeanor, and not a felony. (28)

When a citizen wonders why habitual criminals are not incarcerated, the police answer that an arrest does not necessarily mean a conviction.

I will give you an example. He makes an arrest. There are two junkies. It was a legitimate collar. He goes down to court, down to Centre Street. He goes before the judge and the case was *dismissed.* Now the cop at 100 Centre Street had to take a train to make it back up to his precinct at 135th Street. It took about a half-hour by train to get back. He was walking into the station house, and he is walking in, two detectives pull two guys out of the back of the squad car. And these are the two junkies the cop has arrested! They had been *rearrested* on a warrant. . . . This is not an isolated event. Okay, the time element is a little compact. But this is your biggest problem. Your only problem. (35)

Although each police officer views this problem in a somewhat different light, all agree that the court system is a scandal and that justice and society suffer as a result. The disagreement is where to place the blame.

Some policemen attribute plea bargaining to overcrowded courts, heavy calendars, and workload pressures that force district attorneys and judges to make deals to terminate a case.[12] But without plea bargaining, almost every police officer agrees, the Criminal Court would simply not survive.

It's impossible to run the court system if you don't plea bargain. You have to. I don't agree, but you have to. It's impossible because the caseload—the workload is so heavy. You would have to rent the entire Rockefeller Plaza if you didn't have it. You would have to import people from Chicago to sit on juries. . . . I think they indict 8000 in Manhattan every year. And they have a room calendar time personnel like 200. That's why they plea bargain. . . . We have room for eight at Riker's Island and that's it. Once you get eight incarcerated that's it. Everybody else walks. (30)

To some police officers the crucial problem is the law. It is the law that calls for insufficient penalties, and that leads to wide disparities in sentencing.[13] Punishment is too lenient for people convicted for everyday offenses, and rarely does the punishment fit the criminal or the crime.

If I walked down that street and you are shooting craps in the street and you are playing $500 and I locked you up, so what? We are talking about a $10 fine on a $500 to $700 crap game. So crime does pay. It really pays. (27)

But for policemen, disparities in penalties or sentencing do not entirely explain the deficiencies of the system. One must also look at where the crime is committed. The value of a crime may be different from one geographical area to another.[14] Prostitution and grand larceny are acceptable risks in New York City, for example, but are not in upstate New York or outside the state.

> You get a hooker, for example. Do you realize when they changed the penal law that they had girls coming from Boston, Detroit, L.A., New Orleans, to work here in the city because they knew they could only get fifteen days? You know how much these girls are making? We are talking about girls who are making about $300 a week. Fifteen days in jail is the fine. That's a vacation, baby. You are signing this girl up [for crime] against about $75 a week in Chock-Full-O'-Nuts. Do you think crime pays? Sure. . . . Take a man upstate. First offense. Shoplifting five pairs of pants valued at $100. The man got ninety days in jail! And his name was put in the paper. Now let's go to New York City. I locked up two broads, both having yellow sheets of about three or four pages long. One was wanted for questioning in a homocide, so she was cut loose and sent to the Bronx. The other broad was behind the wheel of the car that she stole. She also had another grand larceny of an auto. This vehicle was valued at over $1500. So two grand larceny autos. She got a sentence of four months—pleading guilty to both charges! That's a total of four months concurrent and this poor bastard upstate got ninety days. (27)

Many policemen believe that the problem of disparate sentences stems from philosophical differences between judges who disagree on society's right to punish, the extent to which sentences deter crime, and the extent to which punishment rehabilitates the criminal.[15] Since police officers strongly believe that the criminal should be punished, and that this can only be accomplished through "proper" sentencing, they can be expected to praise judges who impose maximum fines and sentencing on lawbreakers, and to criticize "liberal" judges.

> What I really resent are the men sitting behind the bench who are turning dangerous criminals loose on the streets. I think judges have to account for their decisions. I want to go after the court system and expose these men and show what their records are on convictions. (11)

There is no respect for law shown by many liberal judges. They seem to have an idea that this is their private playground, instead of a court for the people of the city. They just don't feel it's a matter of justice, they feel they can make decisions the way they seem fit. (28)

In addition, many policemen believe that far too many judges are inexperienced in criminal court procedures, due, in part, to the method by which they are selected. Candidates for the judicial ticket, for example, are selected by district leaders. The sole question considered by the district leader is what the candidate has done to aid the political organization.

My feeling is that the judgeship should be civil service. But among the requirements I think they should have is several years as law enforcement officer on the street rather than serving in an administrative capacity. Too many judges today never tried a criminal case in court. The man has been a corporation counsel all of his life. Suddenly he has worked himself to a position where he is financially secure and he devotes a little more time to the political club. Now, after an election, after he has been politically active, he is going to be rewarded with a judgeship. But sitting on the bench he doesn't have the slightest concept of criminal law . . . and because he has never been a policeman, we probably have less chance of justice down here than an Arabian thief who was caught and his hand was removed with his own sword. At least it was justice. . . . But here you commit a crime and you walk off free. (28)

Even assistant district attorneys are criticized for being so inexperienced in criminal court procedures that far too many cases are lost to the defense counsel.

To start with, your assistant DAs are young kids just out of law school. I would say that the average DA in Manhattan court has probably been out of law school one or two years. And very few of them stay in more than four or five years. They take the job as a means of gaining experience and insights into the court system. It's their breaking ground. But they never stay in long enough to do the job right. (28)

Also, police officers believe that judges do not put in a full day's work. Judges are said to spend too little time on the bench and too much time in recess and lunch. Moreover, judges are accused of being frequently absent or tardy, inefficient in scheduling their work properly, or just plain lazy.[16] This type of behavior, it is said, contributes to the backlog of criminal cases, and negates the courts' ability to fight crime and to support the police.

The cop is supposed to be in court by nine-thirty. The judge never gets in, if he gets in at all, before ten o'clock. So the cop says, why should I get in there, so he goes and has his breakfast. He comes back at ten ten and the judge is just walking in. The average judge in a Manhattan court works on the average of three to three and one-half hours. You may find a judge who is undoubtedly considered an oddball by his fellow judges because he will give an honest day's work. This is also true of assistant DAs who are never around. Anyhow, at eleven o'clock they break for their coffee break, and they will come back twenty-five to twelve or so. Then they sit and hear cases until ten to one. Then they break for lunch and come back around twenty after two. They will sit there until three-thirty or a quarter till four. This is what happens. (28)

All that has been described above is believed by our respondents to contribute to long delays and adjournments, which increase frustrations for the defendant in jail, the victim, and the witnesses who spend days in court while the case is processed. Police officers spend many hours each month in court waiting to testify in cases that will be adjourned, or in which serious criminal suspects will be released on low bail or no bail to commit additional crimes against society while awaiting trial on pending criminal charges.

When you go to court nine times out of ten the prisoner is released on bail. You waste between two to four months on a case . . . and usually the whole thing is thrown out on a lesser charge. (25)

The whole system needs to be redone. It's really pathetic. The victim is the one who really suffers. If he suffered injuries he possibly had to go to a hospital. And how many days of work did he lose? And how many hours of work did the cop lose waiting in court? So you feel a sense of futility. We would like to do our job, if only the courts and the lawmakers would do theirs. (19)

THE POLICEMAN AS TOTAL VICTIM. It should be clear by now that the policeman feels that his life is a hard one. He does not get support, understanding, and fair treatment from the people he serves. He is a "pawn" of liberal politicians who have created a climate that is destroying the concept of "law and order." He is the recipient of a bad press which publishes inaccurate and biased articles about him. He is the victim of unsolicitous courts and judges who are over-cautious in interpreting constitutional provisions that protect the guilty. Yet he is blamed for the increasing crime rate and for lowered police efficiency.

Like most tragic heroes, the police officer is confronted with the alternatives of righteousness or despair. He opts for an exaggerated rightness of what he is doing, fused with the belief that only the police with sufficient powers and unhampered efficiency can defend us from the urban jungle.

Because they work in a hostile society, it is not surprising that policemen develop a close fraternity. Close, responsive, friendly relations with colleagues are a defense against being "kicked around" and maligned by the adversaries and enemies the police officer confronts in his occupation.

It is true that the police officer tends to go in their collective shell within a group because they feel that people don't like them, especially minorities. In my area there is that feeling that you are hated. (19)

I work with the feeling that the public doesn't really appreciate what a policeman is trying to do today; the press is against him, the courts are against him, the people are on his back, so the overall reaction is, well, the heck with the public. I mean, I'm going to be out for myself. . . . So a cop builds up a shell around himself. They drink with other cops. They go out with other cops. They barbecue with other cops. And they have their individual dances and social fraternity cliques among a half-dozen different organizations within the Police Department. (10)

A policeman can almost always find coteries of cops who gather to talk shop to keep alive what little enthusiasm there is for their work. Above all, he will learn from this talk that the stigma of being a cop is not his alone.

I'm sure in your other interviews you have found that cops are very cliquish and tend to give up a lot of their pre-department civil friends once they become cops, and you kind of gravitate to have social relations with other cops. . . . You talk about arrests—usual cop talk. I don't know if you have ever sat down with a group of cops but you are going to hear some wild war stories. There is a camaraderie which is really unbelievable . . . because you have been in a lot of situations that normal people, I mean civilians, just can't understand. . . . I don't think any other people can have this [rapport] because the work you are involved in is so much different from any other kind of job. And, of course, you can share all the problems you have, too. (34)

It is also commonly known that police officers tend to live in the same neighborhood.[17] In Britain, the police live together in reasonably good quarters owned by the force. Rents are subsidized and young, unmarried policemen are required to live in department housing during the first five years of service.[18] But in the United States the police live together through choice—because they may only feel comfortable with other policemen. In England close quarters are his due. In the United States they may be a reaction to inhospitable neighborhoods.

In sum, the white policeman's profound sense of frustration with the job that has trapped and immobilized him, and his feelings of hopelessness and anger in being unable to shape the job according to his expectations are directed toward society and its leaders, who are no longer seen as moral leaders. Society's failure to affirm police methods and autonomy, we suggest, has undermined or destroyed whatever respect, faith, sense of awe, or commitment he once may have felt for its political institutions. The policeman no longer harbors illusions about the manipulation of political power—he has been too maligned by it. At one time his faith in the criminal justice system could act to curb his hostility or make him more ready to subordinate his will to the will of the institution. But now he knows that even this system does not live by the standards it uses to victimize him.

An inevitable concomitant of this denial and betrayal of police values is that white policemen are beginning to see themselves as one of our most oppressed minority groups. Blacks are perceived as the group most protected by our political system, lawmakers, and courts.

It is a strange irony—blacks have historically viewed themselves as an exploited minority group, and now white police, thought by many blacks to be prime oppressors, see themselves as an exploited minority. Competition and rivalry, often keen and bitter, has sprung up as to who is entitled to the victim role, because the victim role entitles the person who claims it to distinguish himself from others. The victim is the most righteous person.[19]

The rivalry between blacks and the white police is especially visible when we consider how the white policeman views his militant black counterpart. This rivalry has not only threatened police solidarity but has evoked irreconcilable differences in the enforcement of the law—that is, in the definition of the police role. It has also served to consolidate the white police as a distinct ethnic group in a test of strength with black policemen over status, demands for deference, and defense against acts of degradation and betrayal.

NOTES

1. Nicholas Alex, *Black in Blue: A Study of the Negro Policeman* (New York: Appleton-Century-Crofts, 1969), pp. 144–153.

2. Of 14,900 letters received in 1971, 3600 were complementary, as reported by Philip A. Lacovara, the former Special Counsel to the Police Commissioner, in a letter to the editor of *The New York Times*, June 17, 1971.

3. To get the facts, and to present them truthfully, becomes the reporter's problem. But whether reporters achieve this depends on their ability to transcend certain corrupting influences. See Joseph Bensman and Robert Lilienfeld, *Craft and Consciousness: Occupational Techniques and the Development of World Images* (New York: John Wiley & Sons, 1973), Chapter 12, "The Journalist," pp. 207–232.

4. See, for example, David Burnham, "False City Reports on Crime Suspected," *The New York Times*, May 15, 1972; "Garelik: Police Statistics Lie," *The New York Post*, May 15, 1972; "Baltimore Finds Crime Data False," *The New York Times*, July 25, 1971.

5. See David Burnham, "Study Asks: Is Crime Cut or Displaced?" *The New York Times*, November 30, 1971.

6. See Fred P. Graham, "F.B.I. Says Crime Continues to Rise," *The New York Times*, December 30, 1971; also, David A. Andelman, "City Crime Wave Spreading to Suburbs," *The New York Times*, January 30, 1972.

7. See, for example, Israel Shenker, "Crime Experts Differ on Prospect That Violence Will Decrease in U.S.," *The New York Times*, May 14, 1972.

8. As quoted by Yale Kamisar in "Criminals, Cops and the Constitution," *The Nation*, November 9, 1964, p. 323.

9. This view has also become popular among Scotland Yard police. See Bernard Weinraub, "Crime in London Shows Increase: Permissive Society Partly to Blame, Police Say," *The New York Times*, August 27, 1971.

10. I draw on Yale Kamisar, op. cit., p. 325.

11. The literature on this topic is voluminous. An interesting discussion can be found in Peter L. Zimroth, "101,000 Defendants Were Convicted of Misdemeanors Last Year. 98,000 of Them Pleaded Guilty—To Get Reduced Sentences," *The New York Times Magazine*, May 28, 1972, pp. 14–44. See also Selwyn Raab, "Plea Bargains Resolve 8 of 10 Homicide Cases," *The New York Times*, January 27, 1975.

12. See David Burnham, "Felony-Trial Backlog Held a Peril to War on Crime," *The New York Times*, March 12, 1972.

13. For a fine review of this problem see Glynn Mapes, "A Growing Disparity in Criminal Sentences Troubles Legal Experts," *The Wall Street Journal*, September 9, 1970; also, Lesley Oelsner, "Wide Disparities Mark Sentences Here," *The New York Times*, September 27, 1972; and Lesley Oelsner, "Sentencing Disarray," *The New York Times*, October 2, 1972.

14. I draw on Lesley Oelsner, "Wide Disparities Mark Sentences Here," *The New York Times*, September 27, 1972.

15. Ibid.

16. For a study confirming this view, see David Burnham, "Judges Found on Bench Only 52% of Day," *The New York Times*, June 6, 1973.

17. Michael Banton, *The Policeman in the Community* (New York: Basic Books, 1964), Chapter 8, "The Social Definition of the Police Officer's Role," pp. 215-242.

18. See "Profiles: Constable," *The New Yorker*, August 14, 1971.

19. An outstanding discussion of the secondary benefits of the victim role is found in Max Weber, "Class, Status, Party," in Richard Bendix and Seymour Martin Lipset, eds., *Class, Status and Power* (Glencoe, Ill.: The Free Press, 1953), pp. 63-75.

6

The Division Between White and Black Policemen

It was pointed out in the study of black policemen that the relationship between police officers is mutually dependent, requiring cooperation. So basic is this dependence that all black policemen recognized an obligation to come to the aid of a white officer even though the two symbolized resentment to each other, and even though each was seen as a hindrance to the other's social mobility.[1]

To black policemen there were obvious and necessary reasons for this interdependence. Although much of police work is routine, police officers are subject to physical dangers. Dangerous situations require each member of a police team to know that the other is going to back him up no matter what happens. Any hesitation or fear from one team member places the other's life in danger. Police solidarity is, therefore, the principal occupational norm in the police culture. It is exemplified in the unwritten motto, United we stand and divided we fall.[2]

Another reason for police solidarity, one unrelated to problematic or dangerous situations, was also offered. All black policemen believed that the average law-abiding citizen viewed them with suspicion and antipathy. They believed that white policemen were similarly scorned. The black policeman felt alienated from the public; the only person "out there" who would "stick his neck out" for a police officer was thought to be another cop. This shared alienation increased police solidarity and helped minimize racial differences among policemen.[3]

But above all, cooperation among black and white policemen sprang from norms of racial etiquette. Each officer became aware of subtle racial cues and avoided racial issues that were found to be offensive and that could ultimately force the men to take sides and thus destroy professional relations that existed between them. Even the intense loathing that black policemen reserved for white Birchite cops seemed to disappear in the face of this mechanism of group control and survival.[4]

Although white racial hostilities and fears were controlled through the interlocking norms of racial etiquette, they were far from being resolved. With few exceptions, blacks and whites did not share a social life after work, and in the infrequent integrated social gatherings blacks learned to sense when they were being rejected. Qualified blacks were denied equal opportunity to serve in areas other than racial ghettoes, were not getting promoted, and were not getting desired details and patrols because of antiblack prejudice and discrimination. Most rankling, however, was the expectation that black policemen submit to the demands of white policemen that they take the greater share of aggressive action toward black offenders and, consequently, the greater share of the risks. By this contrivance black cops could demonstrate their loyalties to their colleagues. The same demands for courage in dangerous situations were not required of white policemen who, as the established group in the department, defined the rules of the game.[5]

In response to these discriminatory encounters, black policemen were antagonistic toward white policemen. Their white counterparts were considered inferior as policemen simply because they were white. Interracial contact on the job did not alter black policemen's criticisms of whites.[6]

The data presented in *Black in Blue* indicate that the main differences between black and white policemen do not stem from disagreement over demands for group solidarity, but from the form

these demands take and still more from the meanings black policemen give to these demands. As we shall see, this is also true of
white policemen. Occupational norms and demands for group solidarity exert an important influence on how whites and blacks inter-
act, but play a small part in determining the quality of that
interaction as defined by individual white policemen.

Let us look, therefore, at whether blacks present problems to
whites by their presence in integrated patrol teams.

SALT AND PEPPER TEAMS. To begin with, I asked policemen, Are
there any advantages or benefits in working with blacks in integrated
patrol teams? White policemen who consider color to be an advantage in police teams answered far differently from those who did
not see it as an advantage.

The Black Policeman Understands Black Culture. Most respondents (thirty-two) expressed the view that integrated patrol teams
are advantageous in racial ghettoes, giving a variety of reasons.
First, they contend that color enables the black police officer to
identify with blacks—to speak the same language or ghetto argot,
and to recognize the social and cultural dynamics of black neighborhood life.

> In order to understand the neighborhood and the people you
> have to put that type of person in there. And what better type
> of person than the type of person who just got out of there? I
> went out on the job with cops who were colored in Harlem.
> And nobody would talk to me. (You mean black people who live
> in the neighborhood?) Yeah. They wouldn't talk to me. He
> understands. He was brought up that way. And he knows exactly
> what their problems are better than I would. And I'm sure that
> I could probably understand something up on Fordham Road
> better than he could. (29)

It is also believed that by using ghetto argot, black policemen can more easily coordinate and control the social behavior of blacks, making police work easier for whites.

I've worked with black cops and not just in Brooklyn, but when I was in the Bronx. I used to fill in the South Bronx on a regular basis during the summer and I felt that black cops were listened to more than I was. In other words, I can go to a situation in a black neighborhood, in a bad neighborhood as we put it, and the people won't respect you. They call you a pig and a mother-fucker. So you can't communicate with them like a black cop can. A black cop can go over and say, "Listen, brother!" If you go over and say "Listen, brother" they laugh at you. (38)

At the same time, the black police officer who uses black argot must be careful not to express alliances with blacks. The black policeman who identifies too closely with blacks loses the respect and friendship of his white partner. To be considered a good cop who can be effective in ghetto work, he is expected to act simply as an interpreter or guide between blacks and white policemen.

I get along fine with colored guys but I feel uncomfortable with them. The 114th precinct was black and Corona was black. The black guy there handled himself the way I would like. He was impersonal and stood in the middle. (What do you mean?) Well, he talked the language but he didn't take sides. This colored guy was good. This type of guy is a benefit in the department. (23)

The black police officer is also viewed as a benefit to the department when he interprets the language and life conditions of the black neighborhood to young, inexperienced white cops. Black policemen consider this a way by which white policemen take advantage of them,[7] but white policemen consider it an appropriate way of using blacks.

I would say it would be a good training for a young fellow who had never seen Harlem before or who never knew a condition

like this existed. For the white fellow this would be good to
have a black partner if he was young and inexperienced. The
black cop may have grown up in Harlem or visited relatives
there. He may have come down there drinking or had a girl
friend or whatever. That would have a distinct advantage. (30)

The Black Policeman Is Tougher With Blacks. The assumption
that their familiarity with ghetto argot would help them in their
work was not borne out by the experiences of black policemen,
especially in their dealings with young blacks. Young blacks used
such pointed, personal, and belittling terms—"White Nigger,"
"Uncle Tom," "Mr. Charlie's Boy"—so frequently that the offended
black police officer often lost his temper and reacted aggressively.[8]
White police officers recognize that this is a problem for black
policemen.

> Sometimes they [black policemen] are a little harder on a black
> guy. They will take it out on him. You get a young black kid
> or a drunk and he starts saying, "You white nigger," or, "You're
> not a black man, you're a nigger." The black cop simply won't
> take this abuse. (18)

Nevertheless, this aggressive reassertion of police authority, this
vision of black cops as oppressors, appeals strongly to white policemen, who feel that only by being tough and aggressive can black
policemen show solidarity with their white counterparts.

> I think there is an advantage. Two white cops working together
> in Harlem will get more static. They will get more static than
> a black and white team. I can remember my first encounter with
> a black cop. I was in Harlem only a short time. I had a post at
> 155th Street and a woman comes running up to me screaming,
> "My husband is doing this," and so on. There is a crowd coming
> behind me and this guy is tearing the apartment apart. He was
> a big gorilla type. So there was a problem. And he says to me,
> "You white pig—you honkie!" So the black cop comes in and
> throws the guy against the wall and he says, "Never talk to a
> police officer this way! Do you understand?" He lambasted this

guy. So I saw the advantage right there in having a black partner. (35)

Another respondent obviously admires and respects black policemen when they act out their aggression against blacks, even though this means for the black police officer increasing alienation from blacks in the community.

In my opinion, the blacks dislike, in fact, they detest the black cop! Because the black cop knows what they are like—not that I'm being prejudiced—and he treats them exactly in terms of what they are like. So he is tougher. He does not sympathize. (Do you consider this an advantage in a work relationship?) Yes, there is that advantage, but the black citizen doesn't like it because he can't get away with what he could probably get away with a white cop who sympathizes with him. (24)

And so it turns out that as long as the black police officer accepts the white policeman's definition and criteria of police behavior he is accepted into the fraternity of blue. But is the black officer who is tougher on blacks transforming his behavior to meet the expectations of his white counterparts, or is he simply exercising his discretion of disliking certain kinds of behavior on the part of blacks?

I found working in a predominately Negro section that the Negro cop is much tougher on the Negro than the white cops were. (Why is that?) Well, I believe that the Negro cop, going back ten or twelve years and bringing up to the present time of five or six years ago, the Negro cop coming on this job had to have a certain IQ. He wasn't a dummy to get on the job. He had to take the same test as I did. He had the same qualifications. Here was a man who was trying or was attaining a certain level in our society. He probably resents as much out there that is wrong as I do. Yet he feels a little more strongly about it because, maybe, he was raised in a ghetto area and he elevated himself. He doesn't want to be part of the riffraff out there. And he didn't go along with this concept of brother this and brother that. If you perpetrated a crime he would go after you. (15)

I've worked with some black cops and some are more, how do we put it, more ambitious than others. They want to clean up their own kind. They go overboard. They want their own kind to act decent towards other people. I remember once a black area wanted more black cops. When they got them they then decided they wanted white cops. They found out after a period of time that black cops can be very tough cops. (Why are they so tough?) Because they have a certain amount of education. And they feel they got ahead in this society without scaring people to death. And they feel that black kids should do the same thing. They also get embarrassed about their own kind acting out this way. (1)

These interpretations confirm some of the reasons black policemen gave to justify their toughness, and also point to the conflicting pressures facing most black policemen: economic and social gains alter black policemen's perceptions of acceptable black behavior, and lead to a lack of identification with ghetto blacks and a desire or compulsion to demonstrate their respectability to white police.[9]

For white policemen, the conflicting pressures experienced by black policemen have favorable aspects insofar as they reinforce police solidarity. Not only does the black policeman identify with the white police role, but the white policeman sympathizes with the black because he recognizes and, thereby, "trades off" the special problems facing blacks—that is, the black police officer's aggressive behavior signifies to blacks that he has "sold out" to whites. But this only operates in black neighborhoods. In white neighborhoods the black policeman is considered a threat because he encroaches on the "territory" thought to belong to white policemen.[10]

The relationship between black and white police officers is not as good as it should be. But then again, in a place like Harlem, it is not as bad as you think. (Why?) I think that in many cases a black patrolman feels a lot closer to the white patrolman than if he were working in a white area. (I don't understand this.) Well, he's in a sense, has a feeling of guilt because it's the black people in the community that are abusing both him and the white cop. . . . And then the white cop is sympathetic toward the black cop because he's more or less a turncoat in many people's eyes in the black community. . . . Now in a white neighborhood the confrontation between police isn't as strong and there isn't that much abuse involved. [They] like to see police there. . . . So in those cases the white cop may take offense to the black cop more or less cashing in on the fact that he is in a white neighborhood—he's not stuck with any problems. (33)

Integrated Police Teams in the Face of Violence. In contrast, a number of respondents see neither advantages nor disadvantages in an integrated partnership. To support their view they refer to small, unstructured, and unconnected bands of black "crazies" and black "thugs." These bands are believed to be fired up by the rhetoric of better-known militant groups, such as the Black Liberation Army, who have been responsible for killings and assaults on policemen, both black and white, and assaults against ordinary citizens and businessmen. In 1971, ten policemen were killed by black militants, some by ambush, while performing their duties. Five of them were black.[11]

Police victimization has minimized race as a factor in police relations, has increased police vigilance and solidarity, and has provided an argument against the prevailing notion held by police commanders that integrated patrol teams are effective in lessening suspicion and hostility against the police.

I don't think they consider them [integrated patrol teams] an advantage one way or the other. They are getting a little apprehensive about it as a matter of fact. The two cops that were killed in Harlem in the 3-2 precinct were black and white. And the two that were shot down in the Village were black and white. They are starting to wonder if it's a trend. (33)

Police commanders claim that the "salt and pepper" concept was

solely in the interests of the department. And I don't think it is.
There has been no great increase in arrests. There has been no
great decrease in crime. No great change in the attitudes of
blacks towards the police. . . . Now frankly, if the Black Liberation Army or whatever you want to call it were really won over
by this concept, wouldn't it stand to reason that two white cops
would be blown away instead of a "salt and pepper" team? It's
obvious that these people don't buy that concept. They don't
look at it as something that is being done for them. They just
look at it as two cops. (28)

Some of these replies may have been calculated to give the impression that white police officers are relatively free of racial prejudice. And yet the killings of "salt and pepper" teams dramatize in a
powerful way how the physical contingencies of police work operate
to minimize racial identity in police relations. But underneath this
apparent police cooperation, a latent rebellion has surfaced, leading
to bitter quarrels that are racial in nature.

THE MILITANT BLACK POLICEMAN.   Whether racial identity is viewed
as relevant or irrelevant to police relations under certain conditions
(the former attitude attempts to avoid police qualities and skills,
the latter avoids all considerations of race), almost every respondent
in this study believes that racial factors give rise to tension and conflict on the job. What causes this apparent contradiction between the
appearance of police cooperation and the reality of police conflict?

Perhaps the answer lies in the emergence of black nationalism as
a widespread social and political movement. In a short time, the
movement has become so deeply rooted in American society that few
blacks are able to resist its ideological appeal for aggressive militancy, and few whites are not faced by its demands to change white
habits of supremacy. Black nationalism has above all compelled blacks
to change their self-conception and their place in society. It has produced an angry impatience with integration, which is expressed in a
militant assertion of rights. In a few cases, it has produced demands
for total separation from whites.

The black policeman's frustration in trying to integrate himself into police work and into the community, and the institutionalized racism that has rejected his efforts have made him amenable to black nationalist feeling. Many black policemen, especially young policemen who have been part of the social world of black nationalism, are resorting to aggressive militancy to protest conditions on and off the job and to assert their manhood.

The aggressive militancy of black policemen is related to larger events in society and is magnified by their working conditions. The determined militancy of blacks, has led many white policemen to see themselves as the new victims of exploitation.

PROBLEMS CAUSED BY THE MILITANCY OF BLACK POLICEMEN. White policemen tend to feel that black militants "stick together" or keep away from whites as much as they can, not so much to avoid embarrassing situations (being rejected by whites, for example), but as a means of expressing hostility and contempt for whites.

Black militance among the cops has brought tension on the job. Years ago it was a pleasure to ride with the black cop. If you had a family dispute you could settle it. But blacks today are supersensitive and mostly dislike whites. You can't joke with them. And you get tired of being berated for being a racist. We had four black cops about four months ago in this precinct and they worked out fine. They mixed with us and everything. Today we have eleven and ten of them stick together. There is no more mixing. (36)

One respondent who believes that whites and blacks should mix together more often, and who says that he would like to know more blacks and to have blacks in his social group is rebuffed by a black cop who withdraws from him in the company of other blacks. This reaction to being avoided is expressed below:

Well, I found that in emergency situations we are all blue. But when I am working a foot post with this guy we were definitely

on an equal basis but I felt myself being white. It was stupid
that I should feel that way. But I felt that I should be a little
nicer to him, being that I was white. I am definitely not the
liberal type. All cops are basically conservative, but I felt that
I should put out a little more of myself to him, you know, to
make him feel that we are really not prejudiced. But it's a
funny thing. I have walked back to the station house with this
kid, and as we walk back a little early and stand outside waiting to go in, and when he would meet other black cops he would
go right off with them. He would be talking to me and then all
of a sudden, bingo, he would go off. You know, I tried to include him in the conversation, to be part of the group, and
right off he went with the black cops and talking the jive. . . .
(38)

Some blacks refuse to ride with whites in integrated patrol cars.
This is seen as a hostile attempt by blacks to eliminate face-to-face
contact with whites.

Blacks refuse to ride with whites. There was a precinct in Brooklyn where the captain made all the police cars salt and pepper.
Then after that didn't work out he made it all black. Then he
made it an all-white team. And now, whoever wants to ride with
the other guy can. (36)

The refusal of blacks to ride with whites and vice versa is viewed
by one officer as an indication of a citywide movement toward racial
separatism.

It works both ways. Blacks refuse to ride with whites, and whites
refuse to ride with blacks. It is all over the city. In other words,
this attitude does not reflect a particular precinct or neighborhood. It reflects the general attitude' towards keeping the races
apart. (5)

Blacks may also aggressively assert their rights to get "seats" in
radio patrol cars (presumably with other blacks). This meets with

strong white resistance, especially if blacks with less time on the job
are given preference over whites who have more time on the job.

(Are there any tensions between blacks and whites on the job?)
In my own precinct we had an incident recently where two
Negro patrolmen who were rookies felt they weren't given
enough seating arrangements in the radio cars. In other words,
they weren't riding enough. They felt they were on foot patrol
too much, and they went in to speak to the captain about this,
which I felt was groundless, because I myself walked for two
and a half years before I ever set foot in a radio car. But they
were in the precinct for three months and they felt that they
should ride more, and the captain listened like the man he is,
like the gentleman he is, and he took their pleas with some degree of understanding. But some of the guys resented it. (10)

In Harlem precincts, white captains are accused of giving "seats"
to blacks with minimal qualifications before giving them to better
qualified whites. This preferential treatment, which is a response to
the demands of the black population to equalize job opportunities
for blacks, causes much resentment among white policemen, even
though most of them would prefer not to work in black precincts.
Apparently whites believe that preferential treatment to blacks, no
matter where it takes place, perpetuates inequality for whites, even
though to blacks such treatment is needed to overcome the effects of
institutionalized discrimination. One respondent considers departmental programs that give "special" treatment to blacks insensitive
to the fears and interests of whites.

There are two standards in the Harlem area. And believe me
the standard is not if you are white, you are right! If you are a
white police officer up there you are a police officer. If you are
a black police officer up there you are *special*. And you are
treated as such. . . . I worked two years, two and a half years
and then I received a radio car in the precinct. But I worked for
that seat! I had no friends involved. There were no phone calls
involved. I just worked until I got the position. Now, just two
and a half years and then to be riding in a radio car—well,

that's a record, right? That's something to be proud of. But these
kids [black cops] are riding in radio cars in six months. And
some of them are not equipped to ride in radio cars. Of course,
the kid may have given them a number of arrests and a number
of summonses—productivity, so to speak. But he's not prepared
for it yet. He doesn't know the area. He doesn't know the job
that well yet. So it's wrong. If a guy works for the seat he
should be given the seat. But you have got to give a guy time
to adjust to the neighborhood. Now in the command that I am
talking about in Harlem is a white captain. He is a reversed
Oreo. He is black on the inside and white on the outside. In part,
this is due simply in order to survive up there. In order to maintain this position there he has to have a certain rapport with the
population. (20)

White policemen feel that blacks get special details and are promoted to supervisory positions because they are "militant," not because they are qualified. When this special treatment is believed to
discriminate against qualified blacks, whites are likely to show resistance to militancy rather than to race.

They get certain details. They get plainclothes jobs and this
demoralizes a lot of guys. Now this is hearsay. There was a
sergeant. And a lot of the guys said he was one of the IBM
sergeants—that is, he had never taken the test and he was made
a sergeant. Also this minority group had ordered so many members to go sick when the regular test came up. So they took the
makeup test and had gotten the answers to the makeup test
before they took the test. This is the reason they were asked to
go sick so they could pass the tests. I have heard about an
inspector who can't even spell certain words. He can't even spell
his own name. There are a lot of Negro cops who deserve a better
break than they are getting but they don't get the breaks because they are not part of the radicals. You have to act like a
nut to get anything. (1)

Whites also resent it when blacks are assigned to special details
such as community relations work, because this work takes black

officers off the street and deprives the community of law enforcement functions. However, their resentment may actually be caused by seeing blacks get higher-status desk jobs. In any case, resistance to blacks is infused with considerable conflict over job status.

Lot of Negroes are getting jobs way out of proportion to other ethnic groups. A large proportion are on details such as plainclothes and community relations. This thing about community relations—every precinct has one today. And this takes men off the street. Now the guys in this detail have a nice steady working tour and make time on it. Meanwhile, the people are being deprived of law enforcement. I sometimes wonder whether they are being social workers or are they policemen? (11)

Not all the special details given to blacks are resisted by whites. Putting blacks in plainclothes or undercover work is considered advantageous to whites because blacks can infiltrate black extremist groups, which whites see as a special problem. As long as blacks are used in this way they will have opportunities that are not resented by whites.[12]

Right now it really behooves you to be a Negro policeman and rightly so. You know why? Take for instance plainclothes. I couldn't be in plainclothes in an area in which I work because I'm white and the neighborhood is black. There are a few black cops who are naturals for plainclothes or undercover work. . . . So if you are black there are many places for you there. In addition to plainclothes they have a group called Bossi which is a special service group which does a lot of undercover work. They are the group that infiltrates all these radical groups like the Black Panthers or any kind of subversive group. And these guys find out a hell of a lot of information. So there are a lot of opportunities for them. (19)

Another respondent believes that blacks who work as undercover men are a danger to the police because they have been converted by these extremist groups to infiltrate the department. In other words, they return to the police not as cops but as black militants who have surrendered their police loyalties to their member experiences. This reaction is, of course, a special case.

I've seen white cops talking about things now like related to the Black Liberation Army and these other black militant groups. And they dummy up when one of the black cops comes on the scene. If you enter into a conversation it is totally different from one that was taking place when the black cop came up because you don't know what he is thinking. We honestly feel that the department has been infiltrated by these militant black organizations! We feel that this has definitely happened and that this is an accomplished fact. (How do you know this?) Well, these people know too much about our work that you would only know if you were a cop. They know our methods and they can set up ambushes and things like that. They wouldn't be prepared to do this unless they had information from somebody from within the job. (28)

The same respondent believes that blacks are entering the department for the express purpose of spying.

It's not just a question of a younger brother of a [black] cop who is militant and supposedly works to infiltrate this group. I honestly feel that people have been put into this job for that reason. And as the standards are lowered this is going to get worse. The bigger the opening of the fishnet the more different type of fish is going to come in. If you make this guy a cop there is a danger here. . . . As I said, I cannot trust any black cop with information about these groups. . . . (28)

One respondent felt that some black bosses interpret events and issues in a racial context, asking how they will affect blacks. He gave this example:

A colored and a white sergeant were drinking together, and the colored sergeant said to this white sergeant that you guys are giving out complaints to the colored cops, and I think I'm going to give out some complaints to some of your white boys now. And this white sergeant told him, "Well, they are the only ones that I'm catching in the gin mills. That's why I'm giving out complaints." So the white sergeant is saying to him, "What are you trying to say?" And the Negro sergeant says, "I think I'm going to give out some complaints to white boys." And the white sergeant says, "If you want to play that game, well, it's ridiculous." But the colored sergeant thought that they were getting complaints because they were colored. (16)

He went on to tell another story of "racial sensitivity":

A guy was telling me another story about the time he drove some sergeants to the 42nd precinct and a colored sergeant was in the car from another precinct. And this guy who is driving is driving through a colored neighborhood for about an hour, and then the colored sergeant says to him, now that you have showed me where all the colored people live, let's go over to the Concourse and see some of them white people. And the driver is really surprised because he was driving where it was busy and it's always busy in that black neighborhood. And a sergeant is supposed to be where it is busy. He did this every day whether there was a white or a Negro sergeant in the car. But to the sergeant it was a colored thing. (16)

Black militancy seems to come into focus most clearly when the black policeman arrests a black person, and when he is called on to support the discretionary powers of his white partner in making an arrest of a black.

It is well known that police officers have discretionary powers in making arrests, and that they have traditionally used their own judgment of a person's guilt or innocence, based largely on circumstantial evidence. Evidence has included general appearance, manner of speech, and racial preference, among other factors, often to the disadvantage of drifters, poorly dressed transients, "hippies," and blacks who have no connections.[13]

The militant black policeman who identifies with the black community (that is, who plays up his racial identity by rethinking his police role) may be more reluctant than a white to arrest a black, or may refuse to make the arrest. When faced with the opportunity to arrest a black, especially a young black caught on "minor charges," he thinks primarily of what the arrest will do to the person. He may justify his refusal by averring that he is more concerned with spotting and preventing conditions and situations that cause a black youth to commit a crime. Of course, this also allows him to escape a situation that is disagreable both to him and to the black offender.

White-black conflict is exacerbated when a black policeman refuses to accept his white counterpart's judgment in making arrests of blacks. When he feels that the white arresting officer has no real basis for making the arrest, or is making the arrest because of white racism, the black may interfere with the arrest discretion of his white partner. Our respondents say this is not uncommon, and that it alarms them.

It's been happening. Last year there was a white officer who was arresting a Negro demonstrator and the black police officer came over and took the prisoner away from him. He said, "You're not locking my brother up." I'll tell you one thing, if a police officer comes over to me to take my prisoner away from me for any apparent reason, I don't care what the reason is, he's going to go to jail along with the guy I'm locking up. He's going to get arrested for interfering with governmental administration. If it is going to take physical force to stop his actions, to counteract his actions, then I'm going to have to use it. That is the way I feel. Five years ago I wouldn't have said that. I would have said, well, I have to see what the circumstances are. Maybe there is a reason for it. Let's talk about it. But today with the element of the guys coming on this job and everything, it has changed my way of thinking. (37)

I know a story of a colored cop. . . . He pulled a gun on two Tactical Patrol Force guys because they were going to lock up some colored guys, and they had some strong words over this but it was squashed. (11)

Black policemen may refuse to support or come to the aid of a white arresting officer who is making an arrest of a black. This is observed by several respondents who believe that black policemen sympathize with blacks in their disagreements with white policemen, thus breaking the circle of reinforcement that policemen should give to one another. In the example cited below, the black police officer's loyalty to other blacks in the community is believed to override his loyalty to his partner.

(Where do the black police officer's loyalties lie?) I'll give you an example in answer to that question. I remember a white cop who refused to ride with this black cop after the incident I'm going to tell you. What happened was this. There was a dispute in a bar. The clientele was Negro and the owners were Negro. Both officers went in. And the white officer took command, he took it upon himself to restrain this guy. And when this white officer turned around to look for his partner the black cop had walked out of the door. In other words, the Negro cop did not want the white policeman to restrain the guy who was creating the incident, and he just removed himself from the situation. (5)

Black police officers may even "cut loose" the white arresting officer's black prisoner.

Black cops believe that they should defend their neighborhood. And such was the case in this arrest. The white police officer was arresting one party, black, and he became obstructed by three other parties who were also black. And the white officer handed the prisoner over to a black officer and told the black officer to hold him while he went after the others. And the officer went after the others and he came up negative; that is, they took off on him. And he comes back and lo and behold his prisoner is gone! What the prisoner had done was told the black officer his side of the story and the situation seemed to him that the white officer didn't have enough to arrest him for. When they got back to the precinct house the white officer began to scream, "Who are you to go around turning prisoners loose that I locked up!"

And he said to the black cop that he had no jurisdiction on the street as to whether the white cop made a legal or illegal arrest. He told them that the black cop was there because he called him to assist him and that's it. It didn't get down to a physical conflict between the two officers but it was that close. (20)

As these incidents illustrate, questions between blacks and whites over the right to make an arrest are part of a struggle over traditional white subordination of blacks. As the established member in the department, the white policeman wants to control black police attitudes toward arrests; black police officers are fighting for ascendancy over the same functions.[14] Whites are not only angry at blacks who refuse to be their assistants. They are also angry at black policemen who issue complaints against white police who use excessive force in restraining blacks.

It just happened in my precinct. There were two whites effecting an arrest with approximately five or six Negroes, and one of the cops grabbed one of the Negro fellows and hit him because he was trying to break away from the scene. The Negro cop who responded on this job, also, lodged a civilian complaint against the white cops for using unnecessary force. (15)

This incident does not, of course, necessarily show that the black policeman is anticop or antiwhite. He may simply be against certain police practices. Nevertheless, white policemen consider this behavior treasonous. The black who engages in it pays the price of being treated by whites as an outcast.

I think he realizes [speaking of the same black officer] that he made a mistake. That what the white cops did was right! . . . And he has been blackballed in the precinct. There isn't a white cop that will go near the guy. I notice that the older Negro cops shy away from this guy too. They will say hello to him, acknowledge him, but white cops don't even bother to say hello to him anymore. . . . No one wants to ride with him. The captain of the precinct had to do something with him and found him a day job up on a post where he is going to school. This is what he does. From eight to four, Monday through Friday, he goes to school. He has nothing at all to do with other cops. So long as he remains in this school he will never be a cop. He will never be allowed to go out on the street knowing that this is his attitude: Black first, and cop second attitude. (15)

THE YOUNG BLACK POLICEMAN IS A SPECIAL ADVERSARY. In large part, young black cops, who are more assertive and more outspoken than their black predecessors, are blamed by white policemen for the incidents of racial antagonism described above.

The new black police officer is usually in his early twenties. He is typically a patrolman, with fewer than three years on the force. He may live in the slum communities he patrols, which may make him prone to express antiwhite attitudes, revolutionary rhetoric, and hostility toward the inequities of ghetto law enforcement. Because he comes from the slums, he may have a poor formal education and a police record of arrests. This background has given rise to the theme of maintaining higher standards in recruitment and performance which, as we have seen, is sounded by white policemen. In addition, black nationalism may have instilled in him a sense of black pride that will not allow him to accept earlier conditions of integration into the department. The young black will not be an Uncle Tom, and thus is accused of eroding police solidarity.

Although he is typically hostile toward white policemen, his hostility extends as well to leaders of traditional black organizations within the department (for example, The Guardians Association), and to black policemen who continue to act in a subservient manner. As an alternative, he has formed more militant organizations (for example, The Afro-American Police).

In some cases, the young black policeman has been instrumental in bringing over to his side the older black policeman, who may not belong to his organization, but who supports its policies. As a result, old forms of submission and new forms of militant aggres-

sion coexist in every black police officer, even in blacks who at one
time accepted their condition.

Hence the militant young cop is a special adversary to the white,
and contributes to black-white police polarization. Our respondents
document this in detail.

The older black cop is a lot less militant than the younger
black policeman. He has the experience of working with white
cops for ten or fifteen years, and he has found out that they
won't bite him on the throat. And the young fellows who had
bad experiences prior to coming into the Police Department,
they feel a certain resentment, if not hostility, towards the white
he is working with. (33)

I don't consider these new young blacks police officers. I consider them militants. (29)

A delegate to the Patrolmen's Benevolent Association attributes
this militance to the conditions of slum life, which he believes, has
fostered the feelings of blacks that they are being exploited by whites
on the force, and that blacks in the slums are being routinely beaten
and bullied by whites.

I speak to the policemen down here and we want to get black
militants and white militants to discuss their positions—to air
their grievances. I speak to black militants and they think they
are being exploited. They believe they are put in plainclothes
jobs to spy on their people, and that white cops bully their
people. And I think they have this attitude because of their
childhood. Time and time again they refer to their childhood
in the slums when they were hit by white cops or their fathers
were hit by white policemen. . . . (5)

Other respondents blame the times. Radical youth groups are
thought to have no respect for authority or discipline. These respondents bemoan the disappearance of the older Negro cop who
was civilized and disciplined, even if this meant servility to whites.

I think this tension comes from the younger guys, not the older cops. (Why?) If you had a teenager for a son you might have an idea. The young cops are part of the generation that is rebelling, and for some reason became policemen. And they are outspoken. I am for the old school where there was discipline, and where you were taught respect. These young blacks think nothing of talking back to superiors. You see them picketing, using profanity, and expressing violent behavior toward leadership heads. (3)

Black nationalism has also encouraged many young black policemen to express alliances with blacks in the community, as shown in their greetings of one another as "brother," by wearing Afro haircuts under their police caps and dashikis when off duty, and by giving power signs to blacks.[15] By becoming friends and allies of blacks, they become bitter rivals and enemies of whites, according to this respondent.

There are serious tensions. It sounds like I'm prejudiced in saying this, but I would say that the majority of them don't like white people and they don't do their job like they should. . . . They give power signs in a black neighborhood, and because of this, white cops don't want to work with them. When he gives the sign it's like he doesn't know or want to know a white person. He is letting the community know that he is with them. I don't think a guy like this would back you up. . . . Like your old-time colored cop, well, he was a cop! Because he figured he had a job, he had the authority, and he was a cop. But today, the younger colored cop, the guys getting on this job, sympathize a lot more with the colored people, and a lot of the colored cops today are militant. . . . How can I be myself when my colored partner is behind me with a fist? (21)

Not all white cops feel that these signs indicate black militance or a threat to whites. They believe that many blacks have adopted a manner of "soul" that they cannot carry convincingly, and that this simply gives expression to the conflicts of the black who is a policeman. But this understanding is exceptional.

What it all boils down to is the Negro policeman has a problem
especially in black areas. Most of them are cops. But he can't
be in the eyes of his peers, as they may say, he can't be 100 percent cop in their eyes although he may be 100 percent cop.
He's got to go "Right on, baby" and "Hi, brother"! This is one
of his fears of not being accepted as a black man other than a
cop. I can understand their problem. So a lot of them put on
this kind of appearance of being one of them. (19)

Black revolutionary rhetoric is seen as more than sufficient ground
for the white to categorize a black as a traitor to his uniform. To
gain white acceptance, the black must maintain a consistent pose
and develop gestures that correspond to his police role rather than
to his political feelings.

There are two cops at Nostrand Avenue and they go to arrest a
person who has assaulted a man for no apparent reason. A
crowd gathers at this point and a Negro person in a Cadillac
starts yelling to the crowd, "Tell those white pigs to let that
man go! Power to the people!" Now this guy in the Cadillac
was later brought into the station house for inciting people to
riot. And this guy in the Cadillac turns out to be a black cop.
Now that's the kind of traitor we have working on the force.
(35)

The black police officer's gestures, manners, and mode of dress
can speak volumes and can be used by blacks as a language of police
protest and affiliation with blacks. The racial divisiveness between
blacks and whites on the force becomes conflict when these gestures
are used by blacks to proclaim their affiliation with blacks in the
community. They also express in a highly visible way their rebellion
against certain police practices with respect to blacks ("I love you,
baby, but I can't stand your dirty ways.")
These gestures include deviation from rigid uniform regulations
and from the discipline implied by uniform dress. Afro haircuts and
black power buttons provide white policemen with evidence that
blacks are not held to departmental rules and regulations, which

require reasonable standards of dress and prohibit the incorporation of racial or political symbols into the uniform. As a result, white policemen believe that they have become victims of double standards concerning uniform dress, since only blacks are given the license to deviate from these standards.

There is a double standard in the department. Blacks can get away with sloppy appearance and Afros and black liberation flags; they can also get away with less discipline. If you try to discipline them they come back and tell you you're doing this because it's a racial thing. (36)

I personally feel there are two sets of rules in the department. . . . There is this thing about general appearance. Naturally a lot of captains had stated that if you look like a bum you are going to be treated like a bum. I can see their point. And then you go on a detail where most of the Negro policemen are in Negro areas, and they would have a Fu Manchu down to here and an Afro would be sitting on top of their head. . . . Or if a Negro cop did something wrong it was always a little less serious when it got to the trial room. . . . But if *you* did it it was like a cardinal rule that you know better, therefore you can't do it. Actually, if you look at it, it was demeaning to the black cop. Whites were saying, well, what do you expect! (16)

Even though allowing blacks to deviate from uniform standards may be a departmental method of coopting blacks, white policemen resent it. Some even refuse to work with blacks who wear nonstandard garb or haircuts.

There is one Negro officer that I don't like to work with. (Why is that?) It has nothing to do with his race. It has to do with his personality and his appearance. He has a big Afro. This guy had a big Afro but he didn't get a bigger hat though. And with this little hat sitting on top of this big Afro it looked really lousy. And this guy was a kind of hip guy you know. He wore a chain around his neck. (Isn't this against departmental rules?) Really, it is. Maybe there was a laxity for some people.

A lot of white captains and bosses would like to be fair so maybe they allowed this because they didn't want to be called prejudiced. They may have been afraid to say anything. If they do say it they say it very passively. So in the past they got away with it. (19)

In protest against a department that failed to enforce standards for blacks, whites began to wear white power buttons, long hair, beards, and mustaches. This became endemic throughout the department, and forced commanding officers in November 1972 to read meaning into the rules and uphold standards. Any police officer who violated these standards would be "charged and transferred." Any superior officer "who turned out men who violated these standards would be transferred." Precinct commanders and division and borough commanders who did not respond to the effort to improve the appearance of their men would face "departmental charges."[16]

White policemen believed that universal enforcement of uniform standards was their victory. It symbolized to them the power of their informal group to control black attitudes toward rules, thus reinforcing the subordination of blacks to the institutionalized dominance of whites.

One of the things that helped change it was seeing black cops walking in with two inches of Afro hair sticking on each side of his hat. That was the beginning of the end because an awful lot of white cops started wearing beards and letting their hair grow longer. The bosses tried to fight this at the beginning and the white cops told them, no good. When you tell the colored man over there to shave his beard off I'll shave my beard off. (28)

THE MILITANCY OF BLACK POLICE LEADERSHIP. Black-white police tensions and conflicts stem not only from "outside events" like the tide of black nationalism and race pride (as expressed by the young black militant policeman), but also from attacks by black leaders of sectional organizations within the Police Department.

The leader of such a group has a special position—he is a paid agent of black police discontent. His job is to hear complaints from black cops and go as far as he can toward satisfying them. If he is to retain his leadership and the support of his black police constituency, he must also head the attack against white policemen when he believes the circumstances warrant it.

The racial prejudice and discrimination facing most blacks in the Police Department may be why black leaders of fraternal associations have seldom been moderate. The recent atmosphere of race pride and black self-assertion has, in any case, further sharpened group leaders' black militancy. But it has also been said that since leadership is a scarce commodity among blacks, its possession tends to inflate the incumbent with feelings of importance. Scarcity of opportunity may force the black leader to ignore racial etiquette, to behave impudently and accusingly toward whites, and to indulge frequently in exhibitionism.[17]

As an example, we can focus on the case of a former official of a black fraternal association. This leader received some power, prestige, and recognition from blacks within the department by asserting his blackness and by being critical of some white policemen. His bitter charge that white policemen "shoot first and ask questions later" was allegedly made in reference to the fatal shooting of a black detective by a uniformed white patrolman who mistook him for a criminal. He was quoted as saying that "the idea that a police officer or any other person could die in a tragic mistake only points with startling clarity to how dangerous it is to be black. We . . . will accept no less than a full-scale investigation and not the listless or languid in-house variety. We also feel that it is only through good luck that more of our members have not been shot in similar circumstances."[18]

All respondents believe that this charge further eroded police solidarity and divided the department into two racial, social, and attitudinal camps, each convinced of its own rightness. Not only are the police at war with the criminal element, they are in conflict with each other.

The statement that [he] made is completely out of line. It is so far out of line that all it has done is help to break down the rapport on this job that the Negro police officer and the white police have. . . . It's bad enough fighting the element that is out there on the street, but when we are fighting amongst ourselves we are in a lot of trouble. (37)

Some policemen see this particular black police leader as an opportunist who looks out for his own personal and social interests at the expense of his constituency. This view, of course, has frequently been held of black leaders when they are believed to speak without the authority of the organized group they represent.

About this kid . . . who killed a black cop. I don't know what [the leader] is trying to do. I'll tell you one thing—I've met very few black cops who weren't willing to work, who were not willing to do the job. They do their job and they do it well. But I think a fellow like [this man] is hurting the black cop. I don't know if the black cop is aware of it but we are. Maybe he is looking for something. Maybe he is looking for some kind of political gain from it. Maybe he is looking for department gain from it. I can't figure out any other motive for trying to alienate white cops from black cops. (38)

The black police official is also viewed as a Janus who tries to maintain cordial relations with white cops, but at the same time publicly makes derogatory charges against them to maintain or enhance his leadership position with blacks. What our respondents believe he has not learned to do is to follow a subtle policy of not arousing the antagonism of either of the conflicting parties, or to prevent suspicion that he is following such a policy.

I happened to know [this particular black official] personally. I don't agree with him in a lot of respects but to get into a private conversation with this guy and to talk about the job with him, well, he is completely different from what he represents himself to the newspapers. I guess he thinks we don't read.

... I think he wants to keep his position as head of the [organization] and will make any and all statements necessary to maintain that position. That's my impression of the guy. Other than that, speaking to him he is a well-mannered, congenial, and well-educated police officer. (20)

The black leader has been entrusted with the delicate problem of public relations but has become himself a problem case.

He's been making statements that he is black first and blue second. From the objective views I can get he has probably suffered a great amount of prejudice or bigotry and is now counteracting with his own. . . . Now I had it out with him. He came to our unit to talk about black-white relations within the department. And he kind of felt that white cops were coming down hard on black cops in the department, especially off-duty. In other words, he kind of thought that special consideration was given to one cop over another concerning traffic tickets. He thought that the black cop was being treated a little harder and he gave some specific instances of this. I didn't feel they were complete. . . . Now [he] was the first cop to make out a civilian complaint against another cop, a white cop, for using excessive force against a black guy. But unfortunately the prisoner was using quite excessive force against the cop. It was like the prisoner was beating the cop up. It took three guys to hold down this psycho. So [he] . . . came in at the time when the detective's hand came crushing in on this guy's nose and he didn't like that. . . . What I am trying to get across this whole thing is that white-black police relations in the Department are not very good. And [he] is supposed to help in the relations, but he is not. He is making them worse. (35)

To achieve and protect this leadership position the black official has had to enhance his racial identity (to meet the militant standards in vogue at the time) at the cost of his police identity. The black leader now fits the stereotype of the black militant to be recognized and accepted by blacks, or conversely to separate himself from whites. This simply points to the problem faced by some aspiring black leaders who carry out racial functions—that is, they have to forgo or conceal behavior that is inconsistent with the requirements of their black constituency. Most police officers characterize the black leader in these terms:

> The blacks on this job are more militant. And more blacks are coming on the job and they tend to form closer ties now. And their black organizations have become very militant and anti-cop. They don't consider themselves cops. Now I worked with [this particular black official]. I rode in a radio car with him He was a good cop. A very good cop. You never had any qualms about whether he would back you up. Then he made [rank]. And I honestly think that some of the blacks in the [organization] sold him the idea that [he] can go up the line . . . but you gotta start being a little more militant—do more for your own. . . . But this is not the guy that I knew. He is entirely a different person. It was never a question of black and white when we rode together. We stopped a car and if I walked over to the person in the car he might say you are only stopping me because I'm black, and [he] would walk over and say: "Well, I'm black—what's your excuse now?" . . . This isn't the man you hear today. (28)

Perhaps the black police leader's refusal to place his police allegiance above his black identity has alienated him from white policemen because white policemen think all policemen should be white. A black policeman should never think black. It is also possible that the black leader must assert his blackness to capitalize on the growing militance of blacks; he may find it necessary to be receptive to black demands whatever the costs. In any case, the police single out the militant statements of the black leader as a primary cause of their distress.

> I worked with that man. He was a good cop. And I don't believe at the time that I worked with him that he was part of this bandwagon. He always had his pride and self-respect. He was a patrolman when I worked with him. He never made statements

such as the statements he has made today to the newspapers. He was just as good as any white cop. What is he actually doing for the black cop when he comes out with statements like: "I'm a black man first and a cop second"? You are a cop twenty-four hours a day. You might be black or you might be a Caucasian but you are still a cop! So this concept of black first I don't buy. (15)

Black nationalist feeling has brought to the surface of police work new complexities and tensions for whites, and it raises in somewhat new and sharpened form old problems of resistance to social change. How far will white policemen go in trying to perpetuate their established position over differential opportunity, or will they accommodate themselves to the demands of a new kind of black policeman must remain open questions.[19] What can safely be said is that the militancy of the "new" young black policeman, combined with the militancy of his leadership, has made the white police very much aware of its own existence as a victimized group fighting for its vested privileges against a strong and determined opponent. In the struggle between black and white over limited opportunities, prestige, and social position, each becomes the symbol of the other's obstacle, and each seeks to degrade the other and to build his own claims to deference and self-righteousness. Moreover, what the white police have described here is only a small part of the conflict, rivalry, and competition now beginning in American society as blacks, shedding the burdens of self-rejection, display the confidence that goes with increasing numbers at all occupational levels.

NOTES

1. Nicholas Alex, *Black in Blue: A Study of the Negro Policeman* (New York: Appleton-Century-Crofts, 1969), pp. 85–88.
2. Ibid., pp. 85–88.
3. Ibid., pp. 88–89.
4. Ibid., pp. 94–97.
5. Ibid., pp. 104–113.

6. Ibid., pp. 97–104.

7. Ibid., pp. 89–90.

8. Ibid., pp. 149–160.

9. Ibid., pp. 154–160.

10. For an account of the black policeman's reactions to working in white neighborhoods, see ibid., pp. 115–131.

11. See "Is There a War Against the Cops?" *The New York Times*, May 23, 1971; also, Martin Arnold, "Murphy Suggests Roving Band May Have Killed 2 Patrolmen," *The New York Times*, February 4, 1972; Michael T. Kaufman, "Assassinations: Small Band of Criminals Accused of a Range of Attacks and Holdups," *The New York Times*, February 9, 1972. According to the N.Y.P.D. public information unit, in 1974 five policemen were killed in the line of duty, one was black. As of December 9, 1975 six officers were killed, one was black.

12. Black leaders of police organizations have resisted the use of black patrolmen in this way. A former official of a black police association was reported to have said, "I'm advising my people to inform people they are assigned to inform on that I'm a police officer assigned to inform on you." As reported by C. Gerald Fraser, "Black City Policeman Assails Transfers to Political Infiltration," *The New York Times*, June 12, 1971.

13. While the research literature on this is extensive, I cite only an early study by Joseph H. Fichter, *Police Handling of Arrestees*, Department of Sociology, Loyola University of the South, New Orleans, March 1964.

14. As reported by John Darnton, "Color Line a Key Police Problem," *The New York Times*, September 28, 1969; see also Paul Delaney, "Race Friction Rising Among Policemen," *The New York Times*, September 13, 1970; and Deirdre Carmody, "Codd Acts to Curb Internal Racism," *The New York Times*, May 28, 1974.

15. Op cit., *The New York Times*, September 28, 1969.

16. As reported by David Burnham, "Police Upbraided on Their Grooming," *The New York Times*, November 13, 1972.

17. I draw on Gunnar Myrdal's analysis of black leadership in his book, *An American Dilemma: The Negro Problem and Modern Democracy* (New York: Harper & Brothers, 1944), pp. 768–780.

18. As reported by Peter Kihss, "Fatality Arouses Black Policemen," *The New York Times*, April 14, 1972; and Ronald Smothers, "Black Police Assail Shooting of Officers," *The New York Times*, December 6, 1973.

19. William K. Stevens, "Black Policemen Bring Reforms," *The New York Times*, August 11, 1974.

7

The Police Counterattack

If we could reconstruct the history, the psychology of a given group, class, or occupation, we would probably not find a "typical" psychology or distinct group identity of common interests, but rather a sense of the individual's awareness of accomplishment, of movement, of getting ahead, or of slipping. A working class, then, may be radical, liberal, or conservative depending on the sense of the individual's anxiety of slipping from his relative status position in society. In the same manner, the upper class may be conservative, liberal, or reactionary depending on its members' sense of movement toward or away from previous social or economic positions. In other words, the psychology of an occupation or group is mediated by specifiable individuals as they see their world from their subjective point of view. Moreover, the subjective experience through which an occupational psychology becomes transparent can change quickly. And this experience always limits or promotes the manner and the terms in which individuals deal with the world around them.[1]

The white policeman is convinced by experience that he has entered an occupation of limited social opportunity and restrictive movement.[2] The pressures and constraints that have been imposed on him by his black colleagues, by the community, the press, investigative agencies, reformers, politicians, and the department all lead him to believe that he no longer has prestige and power. Feeling betrayed by the society that invested him with authority, but that now rejects him as the upholder of law and order, he has become disillusioned with his work.

The policeman's mortification over his betrayal is, moreover, reinforced by his discovery that he is now a member of an oppressed minority or exploited group subjected to indiscriminate attacks and victimization. This feeling of being wronged, misused, misled, lied to, and generally devalued by society is ironically similar to the position of the black policeman. Like the black policeman of the 1950s or 1960s, the white policeman views his social and occupational world as hostile and threatening. He often feels that he is operating in a conspiratorial setting that punishes him for trying to do the job for which he was trained, or that prevents him from doing that job.

As might be expected, the white policeman tries to defend himself against betrayal and exploitation by retaliating. To secure release from his discontent, to protect his self-esteem, and to protect his position as the established member of the department, the frustrated policeman vents his resentment and anger on the society at large.

Three typical defensive reactions or retaliations of policemen emerged in our interviews. First, we see an organized attempt to reduce efficiency; second, an attitude of trade union militancy; and third, an attempt to reestablish a traditional sense of self, order, and government through political actions and directions. All these responses are symbolic of the distress and anger and alarm of policemen who feel betrayed.

SLOWDOWNS.   It should be obvious that when a policeman finds himself working in what he considers to be a hostile environment, or when he feels that he is being manipulated in some kind of master plan to destroy his efficiency in making arrests, he will not work with the same degree of commitment or enthusiasm he once did. To the extent that this attitude is dominant among the men in our study, it is not difficult to see why the policeman becomes bitter toward the department and the public and withdraws his identification from the job. As one respondent said:

> If there is something that has to be done we will do it, but not with the same vigor we did a few years ago. (Why?) Morale. As I said before, you get the impression that anyone above the rank of captain is like, not with you—they are *after* you! They are not after the guys who killed the cops, they are after you! (30)

The only time he does not spare himself is in emergency situations, especially when a fellow officer is involved. He then acts swiftly and surely. But at all other times he tends to slacken and the work slips. The following excerpt from the remarks of a police officer who would like to take more pride in his work makes this clear:

> I've heard the story that morale has always been very low in the department, since its beginning, and believe me it can't be any lower than now. (How has this low morale affected police efficiency?) Well, the call that men will most respond to as quickly as they possibly can, of course, is a 10-13—a cop needs help; secondly, probably in importance will be a gun run because the motivation is always that maybe this man is shooting at a cop, so they will get there quick. But for everything else, from family disputes to psychos, to, well, I wouldn't say aided cases; aided cases get a fairly heavy response, especially if it happens to be a maternity case. But in everything else there seems to be a tendency to—why should I get involved? (10)

Thus police officers do no more than they must, and the less they do, the less they want to do. Typically, discontent or at least apathy are shown by doing as little as possible, not getting involved, and, in some cases, doing nothing. For example, police officers (with marked exceptions) do not take appropriate action to halt violations in their presence out of a sense of duty (although this is what the

city pays them to do and this is what they have been hired to do),
but out of self-interest. Calculating whether the arrest of a law violator will give them overtime in time off or time paid frequently
becomes a major reason for making an arrest. To achieve this objective, policemen follow their own timetable; that is, arrests are typically not made at the beginning of a tour but at the end, or in the
last tour before going into a "swing" (i.e., days off between tours).

> Today I think the majority of policemen feel if they are going
> to make an arrest they will ask: what is the arrest going to do
> for them? . . . So, sometimes a police officer might try harder
> to make a collar [arrest] on his last tour. This way he will pick
> up the extra day in court—that is, make his overtime . . . and
> get a day off for making a good arrest. I would say this is the
> only reason to make an arrest. (25)

Other self-serving policemen express the same view: timetable
arrests (for time and dollars) replace their duty to enforce the law
and to make arrests whenever and wherever offenders are encoun-
tered. Thus the police may trade their duty for self-interest, which
proceeds from their bad feelings and resentment against the police
"system."

> It's a pain in the ass to make a collar. The only guys that want
> to make collars today are the guys who are looking for the over-
> time in money or the time off. There is simply no other reason
> for a collar. (38)

A police officer who prefers time off to time paid tells us how
much money a police officer can expect when he works overtime:

> Spending money in the Police Department is a nasty word and
> they try to hold you down on it. But I know guys who will go
> out there and make arrests and will do it on their days off. They
> get called on it and get chastised on it but they go out and do
> it again. I don't know. I am not professional enough. I couldn't
> go out and make $70 a day working. That is what overtime is—

$70 a day. . . . It's a very nice way of making $70 a day to sit
your tail down in court for eight hours. Or, you can go in there
and get time and a half. You can get a day and a half if you
want. I prefer time. First of all, they don't tax time. (26)

Police officers take turns in being diligent—that is, for the overtime.

There are two people in a car. There is the recorder who takes
all the jobs, he answers the phone. Usually when he sits in that
seat he has all the arrests. And then there is the operator, that's
the driver. He doesn't make the arrests. And you switch every
four hours, once a day. For four hours you will be the driver,
and for four hours you will sit in the recorder's seat. . . . But
if you are the operator and the person next to you is the recorder, and if he doesn't mind, you may ask him I'll take the
arrest. This is my day off. I could use a little overtime. (22)

Only if he has pride in himself as a police officer and in his department will he move swiftly and surely in making an arrest under
any condition. Even then, the atmosphere that exists in the department leads him to abandon his pride, to shun involvement, and to
arrest simply for the overtime.

Why should I bother [to make an arrest]? And I would still
love to get out there and work. I love the street. . . . I like playing cop. But aside from any self-satisfaction that I am going to
get, there is no other reason for it. And right now I just don't
feel like engaging in any self-satisfaction. So you work to get
the overtime. (34)

Even this motivation for making an arrest has been recently
squashed by the department through a policy change concerning
time off for overtime arrests. This makes the police officer angry
because such a change in policy not only alters his routine, it also
diminishes rewards for making quality arrests.

A directive came out a few months ago stating that not more

than two days off would be granted in each year for good
arrests. Where I was very active in uniform I could wind up
with three days a month or four days a month for good arrests.
But they have even taken that away from you! I can understand like not wanting you to work overtime because this is going to cost them money, but at least let the guy have a day off
if he is going to do some good police work. But nothing: Absolutely nothing! (34)

Another police officer grumbles about this and accuses the department of depriving him of the only satisfaction left in his work:

Now they have minimized that good day arrest. They have even
taken that away from us. It used to be that if you made a good
arrest you would get a day for it. Now the TOP [Temporary
Operating Procedure] came down that you can only get two to
four days off a year under arrests. In other words, through the
captain you would get two, and through the division officer you
would get two. But other than that, they won't give you any
days off for a good arrest. In other words, they are cutting down
the only motivation to make arrests. So the cop in turn has to
be unhappy. (25)

Policemen also deliberately fail to intervene or to make arrests.
This becomes part of their struggle against the department. Policemen believe that this inaction is a necessary and legitimate part of
their attempt to reestablish control over their working conditions
and pace of work, to maintain their old ways, and to fight any attempt by their elected democratic officials and commanding officers
to diminish their autonomy—in all of which they claim to have a
vested right.

Policemen decide *not* to make an arrest when they believe that it
will discourage civilian complaints and therefore eliminate review
by an investigation that might prove—"unjustly"—the validity of
the complaint.

To me it's understandable why a great many of the men have

the idea that the least I do the better off I am. I don't have to worry about civilian complaints. I don't have to worry about going out and having to answer for my actions to some review board because I haven't done anything. I pick up my paycheck every two weeks. I don't give a damn what happens. (15)

This nonresponse attitude (or negative decision) may especially apply if the complainant is a member of a minority group. Minority members are thought to subject the police officer to greater pressure and criticism because they are no longer ignorant of the law or mistaken in their understanding of what they can expect from the police.

There are guys who avoid situations especially with minority groups. You know, who wants to make the collar being a civil rights issue? (41)

Moreover, as we have shown in Chapter 3, there is the feeling that the department will not back the policeman up even if he does get involved with a minority group member, so the tendency is to do nothing, or to wait until someone higher in the command tells him to do something.

Our respondents also refuse (or, at least, are reluctant) to make an arrest for acts they define as minor offenses—disorderly conduct ("noisy and boisterous, causing a crowd to gather"), loitering, public intoxication. Even those who take pride in their work feel that they can restore order in such cases without taking the person into custody.

A lot of arrests in which the cops are hesitant to make are arrests known as bullshit arrests. (What are bullshit arrests?) They are things like harassment or disorderly conduct arrests. A person is being harassed by another person and you are called onto the scene because this one person wants this other person locked up. You don't really try to talk him out of it. You try to reason with him. You let him see why it isn't advisable. (22)

Another officer describes situations that force him to exercise discretion in tolerating minor types of offenses:

You get situations where a husband beats up a wife. Ordinarily, this guy may never make a habit out of beating his wife. And now you get to the scene and you decide that's an occasional situation, she is not that badly injured, and if she is injured you try to talk them into settling it for themselves out of court. There are other cases where you have one woman complaining about another woman over a situation. Where if you were to lock up one woman on the complaint of the other woman you would have four children to shuffle around to different places in the city—a family hospital or a children's hospital. You don't want to do that either because your job is not to destroy family life. And also assaults on the street where it is a friend situation. Where one friend assaults another—gets mad at another. And usually you try to work it out where they are shaking hands as you are walking away. (33)

The policemen cite a number of possible causes for the apathy within the department. Typically, they blame the Kafkaesque court system for destroying their desire to make arrests: Forms must be filled out in duplicate and triplicate, evidence assembled and organized, fingerprints and photographs taken, court appearances made, testimony given, and shrewd defense lawyers confronted. In short, making an arrest means "trouble." As a result, when he sees a crime he may look the other way and keep going.

The following narrative furnished by a police officer skilled in observing the ghoulish aspects of the court "system" brings this out clearly:

I'll tell you why cops aren't interested in making collars anymore. To begin with it's a rat race in making a collar. You arrest a man on the street—let's just say you take a seventeen-year-old narcotics pusher. Now, with the fact that he's seventeen plus the fact that there is narcotics involved in it—the arresting officer would have to fill out approximately forty-something

forms *before* he could even get him booked. Now he goes down-
stairs and the desk officer is busy. It's the change of tours,
right? You arrested this guy at 2 P.M. in the afternoon and by
the time you finished it's now five after 4 P.M. The new desk
officer says, "I can't be throwing that into the arrest record
now," because he is putting the roll call in the blotter. So you
come back in a half an hour. You go back upstairs and wait
again. You come down and the desk officer puts him in the
blotter. Now you got to call for a wagon. You may wait an
hour for a wagon to come from a precinct all the way from the
upper end of Manhattan. You are down just four blocks from
the court. Or it may be the other way around. You may be in
the upper end of Manhattan and they send a wagon from the
lower end of Manhattan. Now you go down to photo—you
can't get your prisoner photoed until you have your prisoner
processed by the Vera Foundation. They check to see if he is
eligible for parole—if he has ties to the community. In other
words, all the things that *you* filled out in the station house, they
double check all this down there. You have to put your prints
through. The average for prints coming back now checked by
Albany by this new Fax machine—the average in Manhattan is
about four and a half to six hours. You can't get your man
photographed before you have the prints and the yellow sheet.
Now you take him in and get him photographed and you have
to take him upstairs and lodge him in the pen behind the courtroom. Now, if you have any sense while you are waiting for
your Fax machine to come back, you go up and get in the complaint line. But let's say for some reason you are stuck down
there. Then you have to wait another hour to three hours up
in the complaint room to get your complaint drawn. Now
when you get your complaint drawn you still can't have it
docketed until the man has been photographed and you have the
Vera papers. They won't give the Vera papers until after he has
been photographed and his yellow sheet has been verified. But
each one going around the circle saying that they can't do anything for you until he's finished—and he says he can't do anything for you until he's finished. So, finally, through some
miracle of perseverance, you get all your papers, and now you
have to go back to the complaint room which is on the fourth

floor, and you are running by the way up and down the stairs
because the only elevator that you can really use is the one
they transport the prisoners in. So, this is all time-consuming.
You find yourself beating your head against the wall. And the
correction guards just don't give a damn. They are writing
names in the book over there and you're standing there: "Hey,
can I get through the gate"? Answer: "I'll be with you in a
minute." I've seen them standing there just laughing and joking
and they wouldn't open the door. But you go back up and get
your papers docketed now and you have to go back down into
the court room and have them put it on the calendar and hand
them to the bridge man. You are carting the DA's copy and the
bridge man is handling the court's copy and the other copy is
sent over to Legal Aid. Now Legal Aid gets around to talking
to your man when they want to. I've seen Legal Aid lawyers
who won't talk to a male prisoner until all the prostitutes have
been interviewed. They would rather talk to the girls. I'm serious. I don't know whether there is some perverse pleasure they
get out of this or a twisted idea of chivalry. But if you happen
to be unfortunate to lock up a male you can sit there until two
in the morning—if the judge would stay there that long. So
the result is that the cop is walking around totally exhausted.
The thought of food would make him vomit right there. His
stomach is all knotted up with tension and all. It takes him two
or three days to get back to normal. Now are you really going
to tell me that this man is looking forward to making another
collar very soon? Actually, you recover from an operation
sooner than you do from an appearance in court. It's just that
simple. They do everything they can to discourage you from
making an arrest. (28)

But our respondent contends that all the waiting is in vain: The
arrests are going to be thrown out of court anyhow because there
is simply no place to put these people. As a result, the typical police
officer experiences a deep sense of futility about arrests:

And you sit there sometimes and you wonder what the hell is
the sense of it. For a lousy collar. . . . So when you run into court

and you finally get there after all this bullshit you find that
the DA who is supposed to be on your side is plea bargaining.
So the guy will fly. And there you are with your thumb in your
mouth. So where are you? So why did you collar this guy? For
the overtime? Okay, if it's for the overtime, fine. But if you
are really serious about trying to get crime off the streets, you
are a fool because you know you are not going to get very
far this way. (38)

Respondents tend to displace responsibility for their failure to
enforce the law on the Knapp Commission, on Supreme Court decisions, and on public badgering of policemen by pressure groups,
both black and white. This has caused policemen to be uncertain
whether they should "get involved." Most learn the lesson that they
should be active during emergencies, and "slow down" or do nothing during the rest of their tour.

The Knapp Commission has had a big effect on the attitude of
all guys on the job. As I say, you don't trust anybody. You are
afraid to do things you might have done before, even though
they might expedite the job; you are afraid to do them because
you wonder who is watching. And as it turns out you do nothing.
You are ducking collars. You are ducking situations because
you don't want to get involved. You don't want to make a decision. (38)

The Supreme Court has created this problem. Then there is the
Miranda ruling. If you read a guy his rights he would have to
be stupid to tell you anything. And unless you have overwhelming evidence you don't have a case. So investigation today is
really hampered. Murder is a good example. If you don't catch
the criminal in the act you have got a hell of a lot of problems.
You can't even bring evidence into court. So all of this discourages the cop from being active. (7)

I'll give you an example. The other night, I handled seventeen
jobs on my four to twelve tour Friday night; it was a very, very
busy evening. We had a few men out, a few men called in sick,

we had four cars working on a busy night. For five minutes—at
11 P.M. that night, I drove up with my partner to a spot on
Eastern Parkway, I opened up a copy of the late evening *News*
that we had just purchased, we flipped through, possibly a ten-
minute break, we had the light on in the radio car, it was
dark . . . We were both damn tired from the work we had done.
We get into the station house twenty minutes later and the
sergeant calls me over. He says, "Bob, were you in the certain
number radio car that night?" I said, "Yeah, it's sitting right
outside." He says: "Were you sitting up on Eastern Parkway
about a half an hour ago?" I say, "Yeah, that's right, we did a
five-minute break up on Eastern Parkway about eleven o'clock."
"Well, some woman who lives up on Eastern Parkway happened to call the station house, and she made an allegation that
a radio car was sitting there for over an hour and a half with
two cops inside reading the paper." So the cop says to himself,
"Well, God damn it, to hell with the public, if they can't appreciate that a cop needs a five-minute break like everybody else."
. . . So you know, a cop—his attitude on the part of the public,
I'm not appreciated, so why the heck should I put out? (10)

Police apathy and inefficiency would probably exist on the force
even in the absence of places to distribute the blame. It existed in
1966 when Joseph P. Lyford, in a six-year study of New York's
West Side for the Fund for the Republic, denounced the city's Police
Department before a Senate subcommittee on urban problems for
"manifest inefficiency" and "featherbedding."[3] Police inefficiency
may be found whenever there is a feeling of discontentment owing
to resistance to change, with its corresponding loss of independence
and self-confidence. It can be found whenever the worker tends to
defend the currency of his labor.[4]

TRADE UNION MILITANCY. The police acted out their frustrations on
January 15, 1971 when forty patrolmen on the four to twelve shift
in the 43rd precinct of the Bronx decided to go out on a wildcat

strike, bringing with them at least seventy-five percent of the patrolmen on duty.[5]

The surface cause of the strike was reported to have been a complex economic issue, by which one group of employees contains parity or ratio clauses relating to contracts with other groups of employees; but a class, racial, and psychological issue was the underlying cause.

The key word in the economic issue was "parity."[6] In November 1969 city arbitrator Theodore W. Kheel made a binding recommendation that police sergeants should be given parity (that is, receive the same salary) as fire lieutenants, and his ruling was retroactive to October 1968. The PBA then demanded $100 a month raises for patrolmen, retroactive to the same date, to maintain the traditional 3.5 to 3 pay ratio between sergeants and patrolmen (that is, patrolmen would receive $3 for every $3.50 earned by police sergeants). In court, the PBA contended that the 3.5 to 3 ratio was part of their contract with the city, but the city argued that the ratio was only part of an informal preliminary bargaining agreement. The Court of Appeals (the state's highest court) ruled that the issue should be tried by a jury in the state Supreme Court. This ruling came as a shock to policemen who had been assured by Edward J. Kiernan, their union leader at the time, that a court victory was all but certain. The men were counting as money in the bank (many had already spent it) some $2700 of back pay. This, combined with the failure of the city administration and the department to respond to the background of police frustrations, was more than enough to trigger a work stoppage, or what policemen called a "job action."

A good example of the bitterness felt toward this "injustice" is nicely expressed by a police officer who was an unsuccessful candidate for president of the PBA in the 1971 election.

We had a job action not too long ago where we, as working men, decided that we had been lied to and lied to and stalled in the negotiations, and not having the city live up to its contract. We reacted strongly because we felt this was the end of the line where crooked politicians were too much to bear. So the men in the street got fed up. . . . Lindsay, that treacherous bugger, tells us that we have not lived up to our oath of office by taking this job action. How about when we were told not to make arrests, was this our oath of office? How about the guys in Harlem, the storkeepers in Harlem who put in long hours and serve a real need in the community seeing their merchandise stolen before their eyes, seeing policemen not being allowed to take action? When is our oath really our oath? It seems to be that our oath is at the politicians' whim for their sake. When it comes to bread on our table, the city signed the contract, and they should live up to the contract. When they say all minority groups have frustrations, well, don't we have frustrations? So we had to express our frustrations in this way to show them that we really have frustrations! But when we express them, the door is slammed on our faces. (13)

As this shows, a number of factors fueled the militancy of the strike. First, there is hostility toward former Mayor Lindsay, rooted in the belief that he had made decisions favoring blacks and Puerto Ricans while belittling or reducing the stature of the police:

I have gotten to the point in my police career where I believe that we are out here on the street simply because the City Charter says so, and for no other reason. At the same time to make us so ineffectual that nothing is being done about conditions in this city. They don't want us to work. And morale is nonexistent. And most people are losing sight of what this man Lindsay is doing to our city in this regard to the power structure in our cities. The ethnic groups, the colored groups, they control votes. The blacks ultimately control our precincts, our precinct commanders, our borough commanders. (13)

Next, there is the general mood of the city in 1971 with the clamor of blacks for equal rights and community control, the teachers' strike, and the increasing willingness of rank and file union members to defy their leaders:

These young bucks are living at a time when they have heard that everybody has the right to scream—to do this and to do that. We didn't feel that when we came on the job as cops. We didn't have the right to go on strike, it was just that simple. We would gripe about it, we would scream and yell, we would blow off steam in the locker room, or after a few beers we would talk to each other about it and that was it. And maybe we were wrong in that. . . . But the city had demanded Cadillac performance for Toyota prices. And it's not right. They demand it of no other department. So I don't think they should get it from us. It's not fair to ask a man this especially in these days. So if you want Cadillac performance you pay Cadillac prices. (28)

There is also the feeling that the new generation of police officer regards his work as a job first and as a duty second, and that this was the group that led the walkout:

Within the last seven or eight years there has been a dramatic change in the attitude of the cop. There is the younger fellow on one side, and the older men on the other side. And the younger men, the only thing they think about is money, money, and more money! And, rightly so. So there is a trade union attitude on the part of the younger men, and no concern for dedication or idealism which the older men had. (26)

One of the reasons for this is that the department has communicated to policemen a professional mission that is totally unrealistic and transparent to them:

I think the job is trying to foster on us propaganda that police work is a profession. It's not a profession because nobody has the incentive—nobody has the desire. . . . But they say you are a professional. I would rather have the money (laughing). So if you are going to pay us like doctors, then they can say we are professionals. If you are going to pay us on a lower scale and then give us a title—it's silly. And anybody sees through that. (33)

An additional factor in the wildcat strike is the contention that the police are "special," but that the city administration had failed to recognize them as such:[7]

> I was on the negotiating team for the last contract. I always felt we should be number one in the nation. We had one meeting with Lindsay and I told him what Daley [Mayor Daley of Chicago] did for his men. And we do the job the way you want us to do the job. What did Daley do? He gave his men a twenty-two percent pay raise and made them number one in the nation. We did the job the way Lindsay wants us to do it. We did the job reluctantly, but we did it. We overlook a lot of things. We were told not to get involved, and if we did get involved, we were not protected by the higher ups. It's not a bad salary, but we should get more so we can set the pace. (11)

The police want more than contractual parity with the firemen and sanitation workers. Police want to be special. They want status. Because they are policemen they believe they should get more. And they resent that other uniformed employees whose jobs are easier have been winning contracts equal to theirs.[8] Take the fire fighters, for example, who are at the same pay level as patrolmen:

> The fireman has dangers in his job. But you come down to one thing that we have that no other civil service employee has, and something that is overlooked a lot—we have decisions to make. And these decisions entail a responsibility that could end up with us going to jail if we make the wrong decisions. And we have to make these decisions within a sixteenth of a second. Now a judge has four months to sit and determine whether a decision was right. Now with that responsibility I think we are entitled to a little bit more. . . . (28)

More than this, police officers carry their guns on the front lines against crime twenty-four hours a day. Firefighters work intermittently:

As far as the Fire Department goes I feel we should be making more than them due to the fact that a fireman . . . is not doing a steady eight hours like the cop is. I am working on the assumption that when he doesn't go to a fire he is sleeping; when he's not sleeping he is either eating or watching TV, and then he may handle a fire four hours later. The policeman is working every minute of the day. But how many firemen do you hear of who are off duty putting out a fire? Whereas a policeman, even when he's off, he's on! You are supposedly a cop twenty-four hours a day. He will take action if he sees something. . . . Looking at it from those points of view, policemen should be the highest paid of the three services. (25)

The police are especially defensive and resentful of sanitation men because they believe they have lost economic ground in their historical relationship with this uniformed service. Although the sanitation man's salary has been about ninety percent of the annual salaries of policemen and firemen, most policemen maintain that sanitation men, as a result of overtime and other benefits, make as much or more than they do.

Now what has happened is that we have lost ground relative to other uniformed groups in the city. At one time we were making more than other civil service departments. In 1939 we were making $3000 a year and so was the fireman. But the cop was working forty-eight hours a week and the fireman was working sixty hours a week. We had a twenty-year pension and so did they. The garbage man was making $1800 a year and they had to work until they were fifty-five years old. They had to be on this job thirty to thirty-five years before they could retire. Today we are all about the same. Sanitation is making ten percent less than we are making. For every ten dollars we make, they make nine dollars. They also have a twenty-year pension plan. But the sanitation man gets time and a half for working Saturday and double time for working on Sunday. The policemen do not get time and a half or double time. They get straight time. . . . (5)

To safeguard what little social status they have relative to the "garbageman"—and to protect and enhance their sullied egos—the police are likely to be critical of the lack of training and skill required to collect garbage. This, of course, goes hand-in-hand with their eagerness to glorify the police function, to emphasize its physical dangers, and to attribute higher prestige to their own occupation than other people do.[9]

If you look around you can see a garbageman making nine dollars for every ten dollars we are making according to the contractual agreement between Sanitation and the city. So no matter what the cop does, no matter how high the performance he turns in, here is a fellow with no skills required—and believe me, I'm not trying to demean the sanitation man—but you could train chimpanzees to do the job they are doing in a matter of hours. As a matter of fact, there is a joke going around in the department that the answers to the first two questions on the sanitation exam were Yoo! and Back Up! This is what we believe to be the extent of skill and knowledge of the sanitation. . . . And he kind of resents being put into the same class as this man. Again, as I said, when I came on this job I thought I had achieved something. I kind of find it hard to feel that I have achieved anything when the fellow next door to me is a garbageman making the same amount of money as me. . . . (28)

Unquestionably, the police feel they are special, and feel frustration and resentment that other uniformed groups are passing them by.

POLITICAL THRASHINGS. Since 1898, the Patrolmen's Benevolent Association has been the bargaining agent for the New York City police force in matters of policy, salaries, hours of employment, and all other matters relating to the general welfare of the members. But according to delegates who have attended union meetings, the PBA has had a turbulent history, and its present "whirlpool" of politics has brought with it fratricidal dissension among the rank and file. To understand why the Patrolmen's Benevolent Association has promoted rather than impeded alienation and resentment among patrolmen toward their leaders, we must briefly examine the historical relationship between the leadership, its structure, and the more militant segments of the union.

John L. Cassese was the president of the PBA for ten years. According to patrolmen, there was no doubt that in June 1968, when he was reelected to a sixth term, he continued to command the loyalty of a substantial segment of the police force.[11]

During his long tenure, Cassese personified the tough cop by waging bitter battles with Mayor Robert F. Wagner, Mayor Lindsay, Commissioner Stephen P. Kennedy, and Commissioner Howard Leary. He was especially known for his successful propaganda campaign to defeat Lindsay's plan for a Civilian Complaint Review Board, a campaign that drew on expert public relations and heavy financial support (in the neighborhood of a million dollars) raised from families and friends, police organizations throughout the country, conservative groups, and "middle americano" who saw the review board as a threat to their values. To the extent that the success of a union leader depends on his ability to help the rank and file identify their "enemy," John Cassese was very successful, indeed.

Although to most liberals Mr. Cassese exemplified the worst kind of old-guard sentiment, and the worst kind of old-line union man, within the framework of the PBA he was a moderate. This created problems for him with the younger, more militant factions of his union membership. Too, he misjudged the mood of patrolmen in October 1968 when his seventeen-member executive board recommended unanimously that they accept a contract that Mayor Lindsay and Herbert L. Haber, his director of labor relations, had praised as "one of the best that the police ever negotiated." The delegates rejected this contract, saying that they "deserved more than the people in the other uniformed services."

When Cassese resigned in June 1969, announcing that he intended to work for Mario A. Procaccino's mayoral campaign, he was replaced by Edward J. Kiernan, who was first vice-president. Many young turks in the union considered Kiernan an "appointed" president, and would not accept him as their leader.[12] One month after he took office (presidents are elected for two-year terms) in July 1969, a dissident group called the "Rank and File" led by James P. Kerrigan, a Bronx patrolman who had been on the force for eighteen years and a PBA delegate for three and a half years, began attacking Kiernan as "second in command of the political machine whose leader resigned unexpectedly, while under pressure." According to Kerrigan, "anything that Mr. Frank did had to be supported by Mr. Cassese, and anything Mr. Cassese supported was supported by the men at the top of the PBA." Cassese had resigned at a time when Norman Frank, public relations advisor to the association and a close associate of Cassese, was being questioned about the "legality and propriety" of a $259,594 payment to him by the PBA Health and Welfare Fund, for which he had been investment advisor and contract administrator. Although no wrongdoing was legally established, Frank resigned from the PBA announcing that he, too, intended to work for Procaccino's election.

Hence, many of our policemen attack former President Kiernan as a carry over of the Cassese regime, and link him with his predecessor in sharing irregularities in handling of welfare funds. Here is one respondent's answer to the question, does the PBA leadership represent the interests of the patrolmen?

No. (Why?) They are all old hard-line politicians. There is getting back to Kiernan, he is very fat in the pocket and very well-heeled. He is politically oriented. And they all do well by the PBA through their political contacts—if you look he's been in that regime or hierarchy, or whatever you want to call it, for years—for centuries. He was with Cassese. He was the vice-president with Cassese. In other words, it's just like a river flowing down the stream. (30)

A police officer who challenged Cassese's leadership in the 1968 election reflects on the circumstances that led him to suspect that official of wrongdoing:

When I joined the department in 1957 . . . I thought that the PBA could stop the smearing of cops and the department from civil rights groups. But I realized that there was no rebuttal from the PBA. . . . What made me suspicious of the PBA—of Frank and Cassese—was that Norman Frank was selling himself to the public but not doing anything for the cops. There were thousands of cases where men were brought up for complaints, most of them were false complaints, and the policemen had no way to protect themselves from these charges. The men could not sue for false charges or for these smears and slanders. And I began to wonder why Cassese and Frank weren't doing anything about this. I figured that they must have been doing something wrong financially because they had to keep their mouth shut. (11)

To support his thesis that the Cassese regime was corrupt he describes an incident that involved voting irregularities.

When we were counting the ballots when I ran in 1968 I had my watchers questioning how it was going. And they found out that ninety-eight and a half percent of the men who were eligible voted! This was unheard of. I knew something was wrong here. And when one of my watchers was asking some questions about the by-laws, Norman Frank said, "I should know the meaning of the by-laws, I wrote them!" Frank was making money for other guys on top. And Kiernan was right at the top. (11)

Against this background of disenchantment, a respondent who has no illusions about the corruptibility of those who seek or hold union or public office said:

What is going on today is that other people want Kiernan's job. It's a political thing. By and large, the PBA leadership did a good job for its members. But the very nature of the job itself, the very nature of unions and other powerful organizations, once immediate goals are obtained, the get-rich-quick areas are available to them, and by and large they succumb. (8)

A policeman with time on the job contends that the union is not so bad as young members make it out to be, but everything he says in its defense makes it come out worse:

> The young fellows in this office were all for Kerrigan. And the other fellows in my age group and the guys with more than twenty years on the job wanted to stick with what we have. John Cassese did an awful lot. John Cassese came in the job in 1958 and did an awful lot. Let us give him credit where credit is due. He reached a point where he couldn't do any more. And, he got involved with Norman Frank who was one of those wheeler-dealers who was investing in real estate and the pension fund and things like that. He was using the pension fund for his own purposes. He wasn't doing any outright stealing of money but it was being used unethically. And John Cassese was told to step down, this is my guess. And Edward Kiernan, his protégé, came up with the same programs and policies. (26)

The major focus of the opposition to Kiernan was his refusal to support the five-day strike which, as we have indicated, took place after the police lost a preliminary legal battle to obtain $100-a-month wage adjustment under a parity formula with sergeants. Moreover, he was attacked by militant PBA members because he urged them to accept as "reasonable" a contract that they rejected by a unanimous vote of the delegates in June 1972, virtually the same contract they accepted in July, because they did not want the Taylor Law.[13]

> We really didn't get any backing from him [Kiernan] at the last job action, and I have since said that I'm not going to go out in another job action. I participated in it and I supported it. I tried to talk to guys who were confused about it. But I resent the fact that our so-called leader didn't back us up. (34)

Another policeman contends that Kiernan sold them down the river:

> As far as leadership goes with the PBA, there is no leadership.

The PBA has done nothing in the three years that I have been
on the job. And the only thing the PBA has done for me has
got me a PBA card. And this card doesn't amount to a whole
lot. And the job action—we were told by Kiernan that we would
have amnesty if we did come back, which we didn't get. The
only thing we got was mandatory penalties and threatened sus-
pensions. (25)

It should be recalled that the mayor's stated intention of docking
the pay of patrolmen who struck was interpreted by some observers
as strengthening the position of Kiernan, who counseled against the
strike, and of undermining the position of union militants who encouraged it. Mayor Lindsay feared that a victory by the militants
in the PBA election would lead to a total breakdown of police discipline, culminating in more strikes. Lindsay wanted to shore up
Kiernan's leadership, and help him thwart a challenge by the militants, without giving the police so much that the firemen and
sanitation men would increase their demands.[14]

Although policemen show general dissatisfaction with the money
offered in the contract that was ratified by a mail ballot in July
1972, most of their anger is expressed at the new duty chart—
the actual hours a patrolman works—which makes more patrolmen
work during the high crime time between 4 P.M. and midnight.

Now we have gone thirteen months with no contract and the
only thing as a result of this job action was a worse chart to
come back on us. (Can you tell me something about this new
chart?) Right now we go five 4 to 12s (4 P.M. to midnight
tour) ; five 8 to 4s (8 A.M. to 4 P.M. tour) ; and four late tours
(midnight to 0 A.M.). Now the way it is going to work is *five*
late tours and you are going to lose out on days. You are going
to get less days off plus more hours. This is what they say about
productivity. And all it does is make it worse for the cop. He
has less hours at home. He has less hours with his family. So
instead of going forward we are going backward. And to me
Kiernan hasn't done a thing for us. (25)

Why then did Kiernan win handily over the Rank and File slate headed by James Kerrigan?

The only reason he got back in was because all men on the tit jobs [clerical jobs inside station houses] gave him all the votes. And eighty percent of the patrolmen who work on the street did go for Kerrigan. But that twenty percent which did equal fifty-five percent is inside, and this is where he got the votes. And now all the delegates that went his way see where they made their mistake. Now they realize it but it's too late. (25)

Complicating the relationship between the PBA leadership and the rank and file was the emergence of a Brooklyn-based organization called the Law Enforcement Group of New York, Inc. (LEG) that was formed in late 1968 by a small group of young, educated, and dedicated patrolmen. LEG's founders felt—perhaps more strongly than the older men—that the PBA had failed to represent and articulate their frustrations and discontent concerning overt attacks of policemen in slum neighborhoods, and with political leaders who were preventing policemen from enforcing the law forcefully enough. One of its founders described LEG's beginnings this way:

We felt that the PBA was not doing its job . . . so [we wanted] to get an organization together [to] get our feelings across to the public. Number one, the policemen were being attacked. Number two, our courts stunk to high heaven. Number three, I think at that time we sort of threw in a lot of complaints that we had. Talk was strong that we should have a shotgun in every radio car; we should keep all civilians out of station houses for security reasons . . . and we we should also throw our support to some of the political candidates that do come out for more effective law enforcement. (10)

But the precipitating event that led to the formation of this splinter organization of the PBA was a petition demanding the re-

moval of a criminal court judge from the bench because he was
alleged to have permitted disorderly conduct and police abuse in the
courtroom by members and sympathizers of the Black Panther Party.

LEG started . . . one afternoon in September of 1968 when two
police officers arrested three individuals outside of the Black
Panther Party headquarters . . . and the charges were for
felonious assault and resisting arrests. When they were brought
to the station house a delegation of Black Panther officials
from the headquarters followed them in and they sat down with
the officers. . . . There were about 200 or 250 Black Panther
Party sympathizers in the courtroom. . . . The charges were
read, the addresses of the individuals were *not* verified, three
gave addresses . . . [of] the Black Panther Party headquarters
and this is not a legitimate address, it's a storefront. The men
were released without bail, in their own recognizance, and they
were released amidst a cheering crowd—300 people in the
court. They were yelling, screaming, cursing at the officers—
it was pandemonium. . . . [so] they [the two policemen] came
back to the station house pretty miffed at that time. They felt
that they hadn't been granted justice in the court, they felt
that they had been abused, without anything being done by the
bench. . . . So the next night a meeting was called . . . to talk
about some sort of organization. (10)

LEG incurred the antagonism of John Cassese and Edward Kiernan who suspected it to be a rival union manipulated by ambitious, power hungry young turks who were trying to build a union career on the back of the PBA.

We had tried to meet with John Cassese and Norman Frank to
tell them that LEG is not out after your job, we are not out to
try to build a new organization, we are trying to act as a liaison
between the men and the PBA. We will bring you what we
feel is wrong, because the men didn't feel that they had, and
they still don't, adequate representation in the PBA. . . .Finally
we got a call from John Cassese and says he will meet with
us. . . . Four of us are sitting in the PBA office and Kiernan, the

head of the PBA, is pounding his fists and says, "Don't pull the wool over my fuckin' eyes. I know what you young turks are after." (10)

However, it was not until a group of off-duty policemen (allegedly LEG members) physically attacked members of the Black Panther Party in Brooklyn Criminal Court (this occurred one month after the original arrests of the Panthers) that the press began to criticize the organization as a "right wing" group of "minutemen" who supported the policies of George Wallace, the independent presidential candidate at that time. This seemingly reinforced the beliefs of a large number of city residents that the police force had right-wing leanings, thereby accentuating alienation and social divisions between the community and the police. Yet one of the aims of LEG was enlisting support of the general public to assist the police in maintaining law and order and fostering better relations between law enforcement officials and members of the community in which they work.[15]

We tried to tell him [Kiernan], we're not after anybody's job, this is what we stand for, this is what we would like you to to do. . . . All of a sudden the PBA treasurer walks in, "Oh my God, did you hear what went on in Criminal Court today? A couple of rowdy, rebel cops beat up some Black Panthers." Oh, gosh, my worst fears were confirmed. . . . Sure enough, we go back on the street a couple of hours and the *New York Post* has a big article, YOUNG WHITES ATTACK PANTHERS. . . . The DA's office . . . called all of us down in the weeks after that. What do you know about this, and so forth. . . . I said that we formed this organization to do away with this kind of thing, for reasons that we feel are important to the job. (10)

In general, then, this respondent concludes that critical press coverage, the lack of funds to support and channel ideas into programs, the failure of its own parent organization (PBA) to provide support, and the disinclination of policemen to join the association

either out of cynicism, apathy, or fear, all contributed to the demise
of LEG about two years after it had formed:

> At its peak we had something close to 1100 members. . . . But
> again it was formed by police and for police, and if we had
> more than 325 cops we were lucky. . . . So this got us thinking,
> what the heck are we doing? . . . We started this for the guys,
> and you give something to a cop on a silver platter, and he'll
> take it with the attitude, what's the angle? And a lot of cops
> backed off because of the publicity: "Are you guys really as
> bad as they say you are?" It was only the men in our own
> precinct that actually knew what we were trying to affect. . . .
> It was only the people that read the *New York Times* and *Post*
> . . . that got this image. . . . Without money nothing is success-
> ful; without publicity, and again, the right kind of publicity.
> The PBA was knocking us right along, because they felt we
> were a rival group. . . . We had five bulletins. And I say, that
> was the extent of our success. There were a lot of young cops
> that had the feeling that somebody cares, somebody is taking
> the banner and moving, trying to do something about [our]
> condition. If you want to say that helped, I don't know. (10)

One may disagree about the methods policemen have selected to
express their frustrations and to communicate to the public that
attention should be paid to them, but the frustration itself remains
evident. Slowdowns, strikes, and militant politics are indexes of the
collective expression of dissatisfaction of being a policeman in the
seventies, and represent an effort on the part of a beleaguered
group to dramatize their conditions and command a public hearing.
Police protest must always be seen in the larger social context of
which it is a part, as well as in terms of the individual's experiences
of the work itself. With that in mind, we cannot expect policemen
to continue to work with a sense of commitment for a criminal
justice system that they typically define as unjust, inefficient, and
discriminatory against them. And this perception of the situation
must be regarded, as our interviews suggest, as a factor influencing
their attitudes, beliefs, and political psychology. It is also obvious

that we cannot secure efficiency, nor inspire loyalty or a sense of craft pride, from the resentment and distrust of men who feel contempt for the system under which they work, and which they believe has betrayed them.

NOTES

1. See Joseph Bensman and Arthur J. Vidich, *The New American Society* (Chicago: Quadrangle Books, 1971), Chapter 4, "Economic Class and Personality," pp. 63–86.

2. This perception is similar to that of the trade union worker as described by Selig Perlman in *A Theory of The Labor Movement* (New York: Augustus M. Kelley, 1949), Chapter 6, "Economic Opportunity and Group Psychology," pp. 237–253.

3. As reported by Bernard Weinraub, "Leary Denies Police Turn Backs on Trouble but Others Disagree," *The New York Times*, September 3, 1966. For more recent evidence of police slowdowns see David Burnham, "Police Officer's Analysis Shows Men Work at 50 Percent of Potential," *The New York Times*, August 10, 1972.

4. See Georges Friedmann, *Industrial Society* (New York: The Free Press of Glencoe, 1955), pp. 280–284.

5. As reported by Joseph Lelyveld, "Nobody Could Have Stopped It," *The New York Times*, January 18, 1971.

6. This discussion draws on Emanuel Perlmutter's report, "Parity Key Issue," *The New York Times*, January 17, 1971; and Richard Stone, "Bitter New York Cops Are Angry Over More Than Just Their Wages," *The Wall Street Journal*, January 19, 1971.

7. See Damon Stetson, "P.B.A. Delegates Reject Proposed Pact," *The New York Times*, March 30, 1972.

8. As reported by Damon Stetson, "P.B.A. Plans a Job Action to Gain Pay Raise," *The New York Times*, June 7, 1972.

9. Sanitationmen have argued that people can at least see them working, but whenever you want a cop, you can never find one. Moreover, sanitationmen contend that collecting garbage is the most important function of any civil service agency: it maintains the physical structure of public health.

10. As of 1973 police captains were making more than $31,000 a year, sergeants about $20,000, and patrolmen with five years experience more than $16,000. See David Burnham, "Chart Gives Data on Police Wages," *The New York Times*, March 25, 1973. In 1975, captains earned nearly $33,000; sergeants earned more than $21,000. See "City and Senior Police Officers Arrive at Accords," *The New York Times*, September 12, 1975.

11. The discussion on John Cassese draws on David Burnham's report, "Leary Declares He Alone Makes Police Decisions," *The New York Times*, August 14, 1968; and Sylvan Fox, "Why Policemen Are Unhappy," *The New York Times*, October 24, 1968.

12. The discussion on Edward Kiernan draws on Martin Gasberg's report, "Rift in the Police Organization Forces Tough Talk on Contract," *The New York Times*, January 17, 1971.

13. As reported by Emanuel Perlmutter and Murray Schumach, "Furious Dissidents Charge Sellout as P.B.A. Votes," *The New York Times*, January 20, 1971.

14. Edward Kiernan resigned on July 1972 and was replaced by his first vice-president, Robert M. McKiernan, who found himself immediately in a fight for the union's top post. See Emanual Perlmutter, "P.B.A. Accepts Contract; Union Chief Is Resigning," *The New York Times*, July 23, 1972. McKiernan's attempts to strengthen his standing in the union by "demeaning" the other uniformed services embroiled him in controversy. See Damon Stetson, "3 Police Groups Accuse McKiernan of Betrayal, Poor Tactics, Deception," *The New York Times*, August 25, 1973. In June 1974 Ken McFeeley became the new President of the PBA. See Deirdre Carmody, "P.B.A. Chief Working Way into Post," *The New York Times*, August 10, 1974.

15. See *Law Enforcement Group of New York, Inc. Bulletin*, Vol. I. No. 1 (March 1969).

8

Conclusion

White policemen are a besieged and aggrieved group. They are under sharp attack by the department, the public, the press, the courts, and their black colleagues for using methods that they feel are needed to carry out the special and valuable duties for which they are responsible. They feel abandoned by a liberal, reform-minded administration and by a budget-minded but "political" or "regular" administration that they believe have both compromised their law enforcement functions to satisfy the political pressures of minority groups. Added to their problems is the feeling of being rejected by almost everybody they come into contact with including neighbors, friends, and members of their families who were caused anxiety and embarrassment by the Knapp disclosures of police corruption. To their eyes, police work has been devalued. They have been deprived of their felt social worth and their efficiency has been reduced. They now see themselves as victimized and betrayed by the society they are obligated to serve.

In the present climate many traditional police methods and practices are technically defined as violations of the law and infractions of departmental regulations. The police are often charged with misconduct by the community which retains final control over their work and demands accountability for the way police work is done. But the police do not readily accept charges of wrongdoing or believe that their methods are illegal, immoral, or unconstitutional. They see themselves as the community's last line of defense. They thus develop a sense of "mission," righteous indignation, and a feeling of immunity from the laws they so self-righteously claim to defend. Their discretionary "illegal" powers are regarded as functionally necessary to the task because the technical and legal requirements of the law are often not applicable to the crime they find in the streets. They know that some of their methods are illegal but the difficulty and danger of their work cause them to believe they have no other choice. These illegal methods and practices are the necessary but dirty part of their work.

Antagonistic when they are not bitter, the police respond to these accusations and attacks on their methods, judgment, and character with charges of their own. They contend they have become the whipping boys for a corps of moralizing liberals, sermonizing police administrators, and opportunistic political leaders among the powers that run the city government. They are required to do a job. The methods they use for getting that job done, the traditional and secret normal operating procedures, are now publicly exposed and subverted by the media and leaders of public opinion and used by politicians and elected officials to further their own political careers.

The police believe, basically, that they have been charged with violations of the law by a political community that does not truly believe that what they have done is criminal, but makes the charges to pacify or appease black and Puerto Rican voters in the central cities. Being anticop was good politics in the early seventies, and an effective way of coopting black protest activity. The police became the scapegoat, used to deflect hostility away from policy makers. In turn, the politician became a scapegoat of the investigative reporter and the opposition political party.

In fact, policemen believe that they have been so successfully transformed into a symbol of the ills of all bureaucracy that even those who might otherwise sympathize with them cannot intervene on their behalf. There is little that the police can do to change this

situation. Their hands are tied. All they can do is to protect themselves from physical threats or injury; and even then, they arc
forced to risk their lives, often unnecessarily. As we have seen,
many policemen believe that restrictions on the use of firearms and
the institution of civilian review boards endanger their lives and
weaken their power to control crime and protect themselves. Their
firearm, for instance, has been reduced to an instrument to defend
the police officer's or an other person's life, and can no longer be
used as a means of effecting an arrest. Changes in police use of firearms have become a depressing symbol of the decline of police
autonomy.

Thus policemen complain that they are being attacked for doing
their job—protecting the community. Throughout the preceding chapters, our respondents have projected outrage, even hysteria, at being
trapped by the vicious political system, persecuted by the over-
inflated advertising of the mistakes and failures made by a few
policemen who were either accused or found guilty by the Knapp
Commission, and bullied by excessive internal surveillance and
control that holds them accountable for even minor infractions of
the police code.

The police assert that they do not resent control, but do resent
the manner by which they are controlled. The surveillance and internal control of the police is guided by a set of stable assumptions,
an ideology, which no policeman has the power to change. The personal discretion once accepted has been replaced by "standard procedures" and paper work, by a routinized bureaucratic code of
conduct. Faced with a new self-image, that of a civil service clerk
whose only distinction is a gun on his belt, the romanticized indi-
vidualism that once governed his image of police work crumbles.

Although public exposure of corruption and new administrative
controls on behavior provide the community with some measure of
accountability, the price may well be instability, demoralization,
and internalized anomie in the police force. The self-conceptions
and motivations of the police seem to be negated by the new departmental controls. Police work is now carried out in the context of
the struggle between the policeman and his department over legal

and occupational rights. In the process of social change, the definition of these rights is not always clear, and protest is always present.
The police claim to need secrecy to pursue their investigations.
To expose that secrecy is to condemn them to impotence in the
pursuit of criminals. To expose their covert operations is to make
it more difficult for them to do their job. Thus when the police
speak of excessive surveillance, they speak of institutionalized inva-
sions into police secrecy and autonomy to do what they feel they
need to do. Officials claim that surveillance is necessary to prevent
crime by the police, the neglect of duty, and overzealousness in the
pursuit of duty. The relative freedom of those officials who are
sanctioned to spy on them and to reveal what the police are doing
is seen as yet another indication of the waning autonomy and prerogatives of the police. This means to them that all policemen are
forced to accept excessive restraints on their behavior. Methods that
once made them heroes now make them criminals.

In a similar vein, New York City's Commissioner is currently
prosecuting engineers, architects, contractors and high-ranking city
officials for "taking care of violations," and "expediting" work
through payoffs and bribes. These "informal procedures" are now
discredited as methods for getting approvals, permissions, and
authorization in the maze of building regulations, permits, and code
compliances required in the construction industry. When policemen justify their methods and conduct by arguing that "everybody's
doing it," they have a point. In the absence of honest law enforcement in business and political life, it is hard to expect the police
to be law abiding. In economic terms, the amount of police corruption is probably insignificant as compared with the costs and con-
sequences of political crime committed by higher-ranking, more
respected government officials and business leaders. Compared with
former President Nixon, former Vice-President Agnew, and former
Attorney General Mitchell, and with the benefits received by ITT,
the milk cooperatives, the airlines, and defense contractors, it is
small wonder if policemen think of themselves as pikers taking only
petty gratuities, "a cup of coffee," "meat and grass eating."
Their sense of betrayal invites analogies with and parallels to the

Communist who, after being exposed and condemned, is systematically downgraded by the Party. Having given years to the Party and to hastening the Revolution, he is purged or defined as an enemy of the State. Everything that he has done, everything once legitimated by his peers and his relevant public as valid, is suddenly defined as wrong.

In this sense, our respondents saw the Knapp Commission Hearings or "trial" as a purge mounted as public theater and designed only to overdramatize police cunning, connivance, and corruption. Certain policemen were carefully prepared by the commission to act as media personalities to betray the standard secrets and indiscretions of police acting within the shelter of their own informal culture. Making public the backstage behavior was a further act of betrayal. From the police standpoint, these exposures created a general spy hysteria within the force, forcing policemen to arrest their partners and to destroy, for many, the image of inviolability and indispensability so necessary for effective police work. The exposures worked against justice and the good of the community. At the same time, they weakened the system of favors for services that had been worked out with storeowners, and subjected policemen's families to ridicule and embarrassment.

Thus the hero of the past becomes the current villain, not because he has changed but because his methods are no longer viewed as appropriate to "society's" new value commitments or goals. Once legitimated by the public and by himself as one of society's principal representatives, he now regards himself as one of the society's victims. Such a transformation in image and value gives the white policeman his special vulnerability. It strikes at the very definition of his role, and threatens his working personality and identity. This is the transition that unquestionably brings with it feelings of betrayal: The police officer had internalized what he supposed were society's values and motives; *now he is deserted by those who are the authors of his self-esteem.*

The police feel in addition that their work has been completely undercut. Society no longer accepts the basis on which police work is done, as it can no longer in the post-Watergate era accept the basis of much of political activity. At any time and place society frames a conventional calculus for the way certain types of work are to be done. Society at the same time maintains an ideology that lends authenticity to the professed morality of the times. When it radically changes the ideology, it interferes with the functions of those occupations whose calculus and logic and techniques were based on traditional, conventional, ideologies. Since politicians are now less willing to protect the police from charges of brutality or corruption, it is far easier to observe "illegal" conditions among a now unprotected group such as the police. In this context, the white police today have similar positions to black prostitutes, who have long been more liable to arrest than white prostitutes because they were poor and unprotected. Like the police today, they do not have influence with political machines, political leaders, district attorneys, or judges to get things "fixed." The police may be even more vulnerable than the prostitutes because they are more subject to press attention.

The police feel morally indignant and self-righteous even though some of their members have been involved in illegalities or institutional evasions of the law, because these evasions were the traditionally accepted methods of law enforcement and were sanctioned, at least informally, by the society and their superiors. The society, the community, and the public were often willing to tolerate or condone police zeal which evoked (in the language of the liberal community) police brutality, the violation of basic rights, entrapment, and attitudes of contempt and derogatory language as long as these methods and routines of work were exercised against people other than themselves. In fact, these evasions were supported by the entire judicial system. The policeman's word was often taken as the law against a felon, without regard to formal legal rules of evidence. He was often judge, jury, and executioner in the sense that, with this tacit authorization of his methods, he held court in the street. So the police received the consent and approval of the judicial system through systematic or patterned evasions of the law which allowed citizens who occupied favored social positions to feel more secure from violent street crime. In sum, policemen did the dirty work by using devious, cruel, and repressive methods, and were accepted and rewarded for such work.

The tables have turned. Policemen are delegated to do the dirty work in the name of society, but like the Nixon staff, or like the Communist who is purged, the finger of blame is pointed at them. The dirty methods of their trade are no longer part of what society considers to be the definition of their role. Society is no longer willing to assume responsibility for the use of these methods. In other words, the "new reality" in society involves the use of the same institutional evasions and the letter of the law, but now they are against the police officer in the service of the politician, the reformer, the press, the criminal, and the minority group. The protection of politicians, judges, courts, or the public has vanished. In fact, our policemen tell us throughout this study that most of the laws relating to crime are, instead, aimed at regulating in detail their behavior, thus making it extremely difficult for them to use their weapons ("when you draw your gun you're on your own"), to engage in force, to use their trade language, to undertake secret surveillance, do undercover work, use wiretaps—that is, to do all the things they once did. *But those who investigate the police use all these methods.* This involves the government in questionable practices, violates traditional legalities, bends the law, and violates the rights of the police. And all of it is done in the name of bringing the police under a strict "book" discipline. From the police viewpoint, this is not the discipline required of a large body of men to fight crime, but the discipline enforced upon them by politicians to appease blacks. It is a discipline that uses illegal methods for political purposes. It is a bitter irony to our police that the trend toward increasing legal restrictions on their rights, and on the rights of victims of violent crime, is regarded by some as a "liberalizing" trend. Not only must the policeman contend with criminals on the loose; he must also contend with the law. Yet some officials who control the police assume that this double standard will instill in the police respect for equal justice under the law.

Thus institutional evasions and the letter of the law are sides of a two-edged sword, and can cut both ways. Under the "old paradigm," the law and evasions of the law were used to overlook police brutality, harassment, and racist behavior. The goals of society have changed, but the system still uses legal and illegal evasions to achieve its new goals. To the police, the new goals result in shielding the black law violator. Indeed, the police now believe that they work for a legal order which is out of their control and which they contend has been an inequitable, and capricious instrument of a political attempt to pacify racial minorities. This, they believe, bends the law to the service of political ambition.

Institutional evasion, then, permits a twisting of the existing social and legal machinery to changing pressures of the times. When the need of the times was for "law and order," these systematic evasions were used or stacked against the criminal or law violator. Now they are turned against the cop! In other words, the police officer's own tools and techniques are twisted to be used against him when society finds it necessary to array itself differently on issues such as law and order, civilian review boards, and gun control. Police recrimination becomes overt and the sense of betrayal explicit. This is why the moral self-righteousness is totally understandable. And the feelings of betrayal are understandable. For society, which instituted and defined the police role, now sabotages the police, which it has failed to support and "liberate."

The point, of course, is that the "new" paradigm of the police as oppressed victim is a subspecies of the "old" paradigm of the police as oppressor. As Russell Baker reminds us, yesterday's victimizer becomes today's victim, and today's victim is usually tomorrow's noble victimizer.[1] When institutions and organizations are changing rapidly, the work lives of their members are rendered more problematic and uncertain. Police stress arises because their motivations, self-conceptions, and methods are inappropriate to newly emerging requirements of the job.

Consider the 1960s when the traditional academic was under attack and victimized by his students for not being "relevant," for being too detached, a trait previously considered a virtue. The professor was once expected to be distant, detached, rational, and professional. Suddenly, during the revolutions of the late 1960s, he was expected to be emotional, involved, and socially committed. *Societal values are turned against their upholders.* The police are enraged. They were trained to perform a definite role, and suddenly they are exposed and condemned for doing the very thing for which they were trained, and in which they believed.

Psychologically, the police may continue to affirm outmoded methods, practices, and tarnished or sullied prestige symbols while society is moving in another direction. The police officer makes claims to an audience or public that refuses to listen. And in the present complex political system that dominates the city the police officer is labeled as a criminal or deviant because of the changing aspects of his social situation rather than because of actual crimes committed. But the police officer must change to protect his job and to protect himself. The police officer has an obligation to obey his superiors and the laws, even when he believes that he has been made a victim by the changing times.

Then, too, in our society people have always been rewarded for saying one thing (that is, for having an ideological pose or social mask that fits the morality of the times), when "behind the mask" they do what they feel they must do to get their job done. For example, politicians are thought to present the image of being moral largely so that they can get elected. But to be successful in modern politics, politicians must use a variety of methods and accept the opportunities that might in absolute terms and in other contexts be considered unethical. Politicians appear in one guise, but assume another when they are performing the technical requirements of their role. They are often insensitive to the morality they publicly present.

The police are in the same position. Because they have a moral obligation to do so, they present to the public an image of morality to distinguish themselves from the criminal they apprehend. This stance is also professionally expedient. But the police, especially plainclothesmen, are symbiotically connected to the criminals they pursue. They need one another. The police cultivate informers and pay for information they receive from petty thieves, drug addicts, and burglars. This working relationship, this camaraderie, is legitimate in terms of R. D. Laing's "schizoid split," or of Erving Goffman's "actor-chameleon" who is conscious of the techniques of role playing and of the contrivances needed for a sustained performance before a variety of audiences.[2] Both terms describe dualistic characters and roles. But the critique of this dualistic element in character is turned against the police. *They are exposed for doing the very things they must do to succeed in their chosen occupation.* It is not just the police who are being attacked, therefore; it is their professional role that is being attacked.

Seen in this light, then, this is a study of the dualistic character of work which is necessary for the functioning of society. The police have been "hoisted on their own petard." This dual character role operates at all levels of society, from the highest government official to the lowest civil servant bureaucrat. And this is a case study of the dual character role being attacked at the lowest level.

Of course, once their conduct invites social condemnation, and personal stigma is attached to their methods, the police respond like a besieged garrision with little help or relief. Their response reflects a demoralization based on their sense of betrayal. They cut down on their work. They coop on the job. They go out on strike. They participate in quasi-violent demonstrations reminiscent of populist movements, striking a virtuous pose that they are victims of their own virtues rather than of their indiscretions. And they develop a defensive solidarity with other police who share and make a culture out of their sense of victimization, a solidarity that expresses a kindred enmity toward all who fail to support and respect them. They have little power to change what they do not like, but enough to resist change when they feel it undermines their special and valuable position to protect the community and to maintain law and order. Their only justification is the thought that they are needed: Their country is threatened by violence and the only defense is the police.

How do policemen respond to the charge that they coop, and fail to put in a respectable day's work? Their self-justification, based on the necessity of their function, would appear to contradict "goofing off." But under the present circumstances they feel that apprehending criminals and making arrests is not only more trouble than it is worth, it is dangerous. To maintain law and order, it is felt that force must be used against people who resist arrest for crimes that require police action. The argument goes that if they are going to be exposed for using this force, it is foolish to make the arrest. From their point of view, if you cannot function effectively, why function at all? You are not rewarded for doing your job; you are punished for it. In short, policemen are afraid to do their job. They are afraid to use their weapon and afraid to act without it. Cooping, goofing off, then, is not simply idleness, it is a form of withdrawal from an intolerable situation.

So like the Nixon staff, the police are obsessed with being under investigation. They are under attack; they are subject to great pressure; and they try to find ways to cover up or protect themselves against being undone or betrayed. The police function has shifted entirely to the function of professional survival. Policemen no longer put their major energy, skill, and courage into making arrests. They put it into not being caught in their own "crimes."

Like other self-righteous groups in society that feel betrayed, the police feel they alone promote the "true" values of the society. Things would return to normal, if they could only stop the liberals, the social critics, and the press who are making it impossible for them to function. If they could regain their prerogatives and their old ways of doing things. If people would accept and truly respect their work and authority. If their superiors would only ignore all the unsubstantiated civilian complaints they receive. If they would only stop investigating the police, then we could see an increase in law and order. Like Nixon staff members who justified their illegality by the belief that they were preventing a radical take-over by McGovern and by referring to what used to be called a "higher duty" than obeying the law, the police define their immorality and "criminal" conduct in terms of protecting American society from the dark corners of crime and violence. It is the police who put their lives on the line to protect our sense of security. If there is any dishonor attached to police work, society should stand ready to assume responsibility for it.

Unfortunately, what the police seem to overlook is that there are two types of "crime" as revealed by both the Knapp Commission and the early demands for civilian review to investigate allegations of police misconduct. The Knapp Commission focused, for instance, on payoffs, bribery, and actual cooperation with criminals in the commission of crime. These crimes are quite different from police brutality, the use of illegal surveillance, wiretaps, entrapment, and illegal search and seizure. The first type of crime is a direct violation or negation of the law; that is, the police acting as ordinary criminals. The second type is caused by an inappropriate excess of zeal; that is, using illegal methods in the exercise of their trade. The police seem to confuse the two, and use the arguments directed against excess of duty to cover up purely criminal activity. The third type of crime—goofing off, cooping, neglect of duty or failure to make arrests—is a response to demoralization.

The Police Department and its political supporters originally glorified the police function. Its importance in maintaining law and order and the risks involved were touted to create morale, esprit de corps, and to compensate for poor pay. Teaching pride in a job well done was overlooked. The drive to professionalize police work was aimed at providing a motivational anchor for the police role, but this propaganda was taken too seriously by policemen. Policemen began to confuse the importance of their function with their importance as individuals. By internalizing or believing in their own public relations, they have come to believe that they are all-important for society, and have become self-righteous. What the police perhaps fail to understand is that important functions can be carried out by unimportant people. The sanitation workers are right, they probably do exercise even more important functions to society than do policemen.

The overemphasis on self-righteousness has resulted in a sense of being above the law as evidenced by their demanding and accepting illegal exactions for the exercise of their trade; using illegal methods in the exercise of their trade; and using the police function and their standards of right in the struggle for ethnic predominance.

Here, in this latter sense, the police take a self-righteous stand and say it is better to be true to "standards" on the job than to those standards that allow blacks to represent themselves falsely as policemen. They argue that if the political officials who control the police would only stop the steady stream of unqualified black and Puerto Ricans who are joining their ranks, the white ethnic could do a better job. After all, the police contend, the politicians are bringing the opposition into the department. They are bringing in their natural enemies, people from the pool of criminals. And this tarnishes the police image and makes the police less effective because the public has less trust in them. The police need help from the public. Who is going to help the police if they think all policemen are criminals!

As we have seen, some white policemen feel that black police cadets show no discipline. They seem to have no respect for sacred places like the Police Academy, which reveals the essence of police professionalism, nor respect for the rules regarding private property, decorum, protocol, dress, or professional etiquette. Convinced of their rightness, white policemen are particularly incensed at the lack of submissiveness and gratitude that their new black co-workers reveal. The new black policemen are less servile than those in the past. They are no longer "exceptions." They are viewed and characterized as militants and troublemakers. They discredit the police when dealing with black offenders, or they interfere with white policemen making arrests. They even castigate or embarrass their white colleagues in public. This undermines white cops' social expectations and trust in the black officer's professional responsibility, integrity, and competence. Black policemen are viewed as renegades who cannot be trusted or controlled. The attempt to monopolize what little opportunity and privilege whites have as the established group in the department has been effectively challenged by the "invasion" of black patrolmen into their ranks; and this, they believe, has eroded the prestige and professionalism of the job. The attraction of police work for blacks was a function of opportunities for social mobility as police officers—becoming police officers meant a certain amount of liberation from their old positions. For white police officers, mobility is a thing of the past because blacks have devalued their job and their social currency in the community. It is because they have become policemen that white policemen have all this trouble. The only way to assure them that they are not betrayed from within, they feel, is to limit the number of blacks who join their ranks. The latter all but fail to meet the standards anyway. The fewer the blacks, the less chance of treachery.

The "decline in standards" is, of course, a euphemism, a catchword used by the white police that conceals the unpleasant realities of black entrance into police work, and of reversals of the advantages created for whites by past discrimination against blacks. The phrase overstates the case of whites that they are, in some mysterious way, an exception to the decline in standards. In other words, the white police are trying to impress us with their ideal motives and their unique qualifications and ability in police work.

Yet we find that many whites entered the job for no apparent specific reason. They simply "drifted" into the job without having any clear career preference or self-directed occupational commitment to police work. They became policemen presumably because of the ease of entry that police work entailed (that is, because of the decline in standards of entry). And they acquired their self-righteousness only after they were on the job. Then they "reassessed" their own motives, reading the higher motives into their decision to enter the force. This means that the righteousness that combined with and led to images of racial and ethnic superiority is the unintended by-product of police education and public relations, which were designed to create morale and esprit de corps. The rhetoric and pageantry of police education and public relations is *misapplied* by the police to support the impression that the white police officer is somehow set apart from the black inside and outside the police force. The politics of prestige requires that they not work with blacks under conditions of equality.

Finally, the reality of being a policeman is substantially different from what many policemen expected and wished for. Those who wanted to get out of the lower class do not escape their past.

Their past comes up to haunt them in the form of public devaluation of police work. They have not graduated from this image. This is particularly true for those who entered the force because they wanted a secure job or to be thought of as respected members of society. Instead, they find that they are viewed as criminals, treated as outcasts, and criticized for not doing enough.

But the major crime of the white policeman may well have been the betrayal of his own ideology—to protect life and property, to prevent lawlessness, and to apprehend the lawbreaker. For if he believed he had a special function—a mission—then he would be obligated to accept its own imperatives; that is, the restraints that his professional position ought to give him. This might entitle him to some overstepping of the boundaries of the law. But in addition to being attacked for excess of duty, he is also attacked for succumbing to corrupt influences and practices.

When combined with a decline in work productivity, the white police officer's new militancy—his demands for greater pay, for more autonomy, for ethnic superiority, and for exemption from the law—is the ultimate betrayal. The policeman is not only betrayed by others, he unknowingly betrays himself.

NOTES

1. Russell Baker, "Noble Causes Need Happy Victims," *The New York Times Magazine,* August 12, 1973.
2. See R. D. Laing, *The Divided Self* (New York: Pantheon Books, 1969) ; and Erving Goffman, *The Presentation of Self in Everyday Life* (Garden City: N.Y.: Doubleday Anchor Books, 1959).

Index of Respondents

Index of Subjects

All agencies and departments are part of the New York Police Department or the New York City government. All police service organizations are of members of the New York Police Department.